YESTERDAY'S

1870 — 1910

TORONTO

Edited by Linda Shapiro

Coles Looking Back Series

ISBN 0~7740~2678~2

© COPYRIGHT 1978 AND PUBLISHED BY
COLES PUBLISHING COMPANY LIMITED
TORONTO — CANADA
PRINTED IN CANADA

To all those
who lived
the original

CONTENTS

Acknowledgements..viii

Introduction..ix

1 Where we walked 1

2 Where we worked 47

3 Where we played 71

4 How we got there 105

5 How we lived 127

Photographic Sources...................................148

Bibliography...149

Acknowledgements

A sincere and special thank you to The City of Toronto Archives, the Canadian History Department of the Metropolitan Toronto Library, Jeffrey Cole and the publisher's artists and designers.

Introduction

The photographs and words in *Yesterday's Toronto* take us into the world of our city from 1870 to 1910. We become eyewitnesses to 40 years of events and emotions. We are removed from our daily routine and thrust into an era when things were very different.

Very few of those *good old days* had reliable cars, traffic lights, telephones, movies, central heating or divorce courts. None of those days had televisions, jet airplanes, subways, air conditioning, expressways or electrical appliances.

Ladies wore corsets under their hoopskirts and carried parasols to protect them from the sun. Gentlemen wore bowler hats, baggy pants and never took off their jackets in public. When crossing a busy road, a proper gentleman always held his lady's elbow and respectable people were never seen walking the streets after 11:00 p.m.

Women were not allowed to vote. There were few trade unions and no minimum wage laws, unemployment insurance, old age pension, welfare, baby bonuses or medical health insurance plans.

Crimes of the day included highway robbery, pickpocketing and trying to enjoy yourself on Sunday, the day on which absolutely nothing was allowed.

And talk about prices! A house on Charles Street sold for $3,200. Ladies' boots were $1 a pair. Taxis were $1 an hour. One-speed bicycles cost $100 each. The price of mailing a letter anywhere in Canada was 1¢. Oranges were 2 dozen for 25¢. The King Edward Hotel charged 15¢ for a liquor drink and 85¢ for a sirloin steak. The best hotels cost $4 per night and would often send an elegant horse and carriage to meet their valued guests at the railway station.

Average yearly salaries included $2,000 for the Mayor, $355 for factory workers, $720 for male teachers and $324 for female teachers.

Well- and little-known facts such as these are blended with the photographs and illustrate aspects of our city's evolution. For the most part, this information has been taken from the writings of Toronto authors and commentators of the period.

In Chapter 1, *Where We Walked*, we travel the muddy roads up Yonge Street, the longest street in the world, to the wilderness of York Mills. En route, we pass the water trough at the corner of College and Spadina, the log cabin at the corner of Bloor and Avenue Road, the Pioneer Hotel at Bloor and Bathurst Streets, young boys skinny dipping in the Don River, McCaul's Pond on the University of Toronto campus and a woman milking a cow in a field at Eglinton and Yonge.

In Chapter 2, *Where We Worked*, we see the toil and the tears that went into making our city what it is today. While some people worked in clean, comfortable offices and stores, other people laboured under treacherous conditions building sewers, constructing streetcar tracks, sewing in sweatshops and peddling rags, while many men and women couldn't find any work at all.

In Chapter 3, *Where We Played*, we watch Torontonians having fun. Swimming and boating at the Island, strolling along the Sunnyside Boardwalk, skiing and snuggling in High Park, playing baseball at Christie Pits, playing the horses at the track, partying at Fort York and car racing at the CNE were some of the things that yesterday's good clean fun were made of.

In Chapter 4, *How We Got There*, we trudge through the mud and shoulder-high snow in a horse and wagon. We lumber along from the St. Lawrence Market to Woodbine Park in a two-horse horsecar at the speed of six miles per hour for the price of 25¢. We exasperatingly push our brand new motorcar up a hill, and then sadly resort to our old reliable horse, bicycle or feet.

In Chapter 5, *How We Lived*, we re-live the local and world events which touched our souls and remained forever a part of our city's history. How can we ever forget the devastating Toronto Fire of 1904, Queen Victoria's Jubilee celebrations, Toronto's soldiers marching off to South Africa, our slum children searching for homes, the paralyzing snow storm of 1896 and our very own fly swatting contest?

Yesterday's Toronto, 1870-1910, is a *human* history of the city intended to give us an appreciation and an awareness of where we came from.

1

Where we walked

It was the best of times, it was the worst of times, it was the age of wisdom, it was the age of foolishness, it was the epoch of belief, it was the epoch of incredulity, it was the season of Light, it was the season of Darkness, it was the spring of hope, it was the winter of despair, we had everything before us, we had nothing before us, we were all going direct to Heaven, we were all going direct the other way — in short, the period was so far like the present period.

from Charles Dickens, *A Tale of Two Cities*, 1859.

Yonge Street looking north from King Street, 1901.

In the early 1800's, all kinds of inns lined both sides of King, Queen and Yonge Streets beginning at the waterfront and stretching northwards. Anticipating the needs of the weary traveller who had braved the muddy roads from Niagara to Kingston became a very profitable business. On King Street West also stood Toronto's first jail and courthouse. In the jailyard, evil-doers were exposed to the ridicule of the passers-by and the condemned were publicly executed.

King Street looking east from Yonge Street, 1873.

In May, 1842, Charles Dickens described Toronto as "full of life, motion, business and improvement. The streets are well-paved and lighted with gas."

Toronto emerged from darkness into light in 1841 when 100 gas lamps were turned on for the city's 16,000 citizens. The first experimental electric lighting occurred in 1879 at McConkey's Restaurant on King Street West. Free ice cream was served until 9:00 p.m. to celebrate the incredible demonstration. In 1911, Toronto said goodnight and goodbye to the gas era and electricity came into use for street lighting as well as general household needs.

Yonge Street looking south from King Street, 1875.

5

From the very earliest days of *Muddy Little York*, the south side of King was the sight of the most showy places of business. There, an Italian confectioner dispensed ice cream to the officers of the garrison and to ladies of fashion. Today, King Street is the oldest, the most historic, the stateliest and most beautiful of Toronto streets. Here are restaurants where men and ladies dine as luxuriously as in New York or London. Is there any taste you desire to gratify? O reader, put money in thy purse and take a walk along the south side of King Street. No Canadian city, not even Montreal, possesses a nobler conjunction of four great streets than that of Yonge and King.

from C.P. Mulvany, *Toronto Past and Present*, 1884.

Yonge Street south of King Street, 1890. (above)

King Street East, between Yonge and Church Streets, 1904. (below)

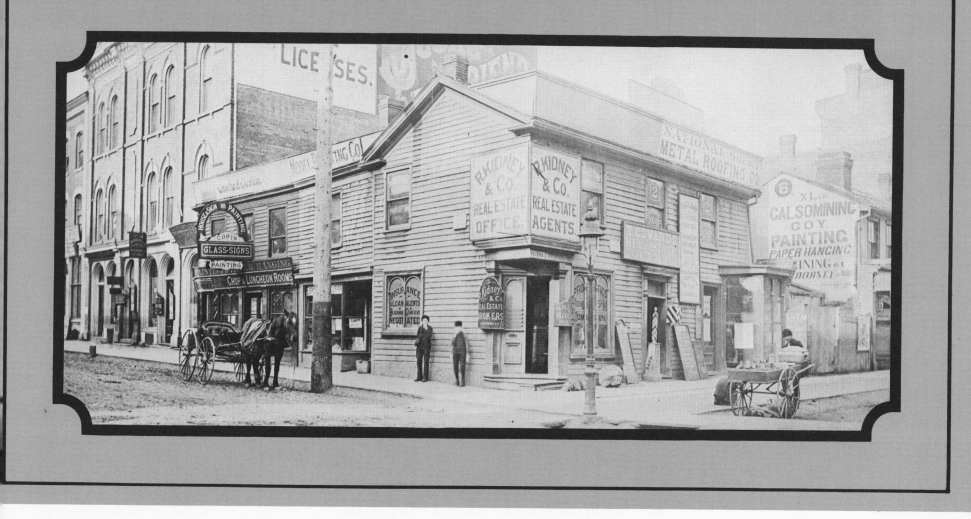

On this enterprising street corner, you could arrange to buy property, pick up a marriage license, negotiate a loan, buy some insurance, plan to have your roof fixed and house papered and painted, eat lunch, and even get your hair cut!

The northwest corner of Adelaide and Victoria Streets, the site of the Cavan Arms Hotel, built in 1825 by Mathew Walton, 1888.

Soon after this photograph was taken, the corner was demolished to make way for the new Simpson's building constructed in 1899.

Street etiquette dictates that in crossing the street, a lady should gracefully raise her dress a little above her ankle with one hand. To raise the dress with both hands is vulgar, except in places where the mud is very deep.

from G. Nichols, *The Great Nineteenth Century Household Guide*, 1894.

At night, the streets, especially Yonge and Queen, are crowded with people of both sexes and the promenade is kept up until nearly eleven when the streets become entirely deserted.

from C.S. Clark, *Of Toronto The Good*, 1898.

The northwest corner of Yonge and Richmond Streets, 1899.

Catarrh is a dreaded disease felt in every household. It is insidious developing into stages of consumption until death releases its victim. To Messrs. A.H. Dixon and Son must be awarded the wreath of bay for a discovery that roots out this curse and his name must endure forever.

from C.P. Mulvany, *Toronto Past and Present*, 1884.

As a general rule, medicines advertised as panaceas for ills are humbugs and utterly worthless. Many are made of harmless drugs which do no harm and no good; but others are composed of dangerous substances. The hair dyes advertised contain poison. The ointment for promoting growth of whiskers and mustaches is either perfumed or coloured lard.

from C.S. Clark, *Of Toronto the Good*, 1898.

Yonge Street from Richmond Street to Queen Street, 1890.

The Globe, on sale at corner news-stands for 3¢, strongly supported the campaign to make Toronto a city where neither streetcars, nor people, nor almost anything operated on Sundays. The paper also championed the cause of abstinence and the city news columns were self-righteously brimming with reports of drunkeness, disorderly conduct, and stiff fines. Ironically, George Brown, the *Globe's* founder was shot to death in 1880 by George Bennett, a drunken engine-room employee whom he had fired because of excessive drinking. Mr. Bennett was promptly hanged.

The northeast corner of Yonge and Shuter Streets, 1908.

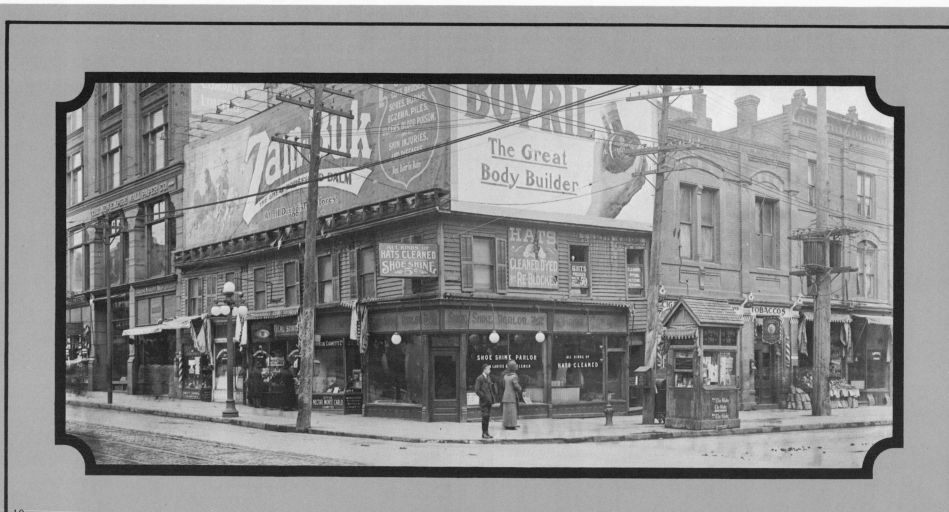

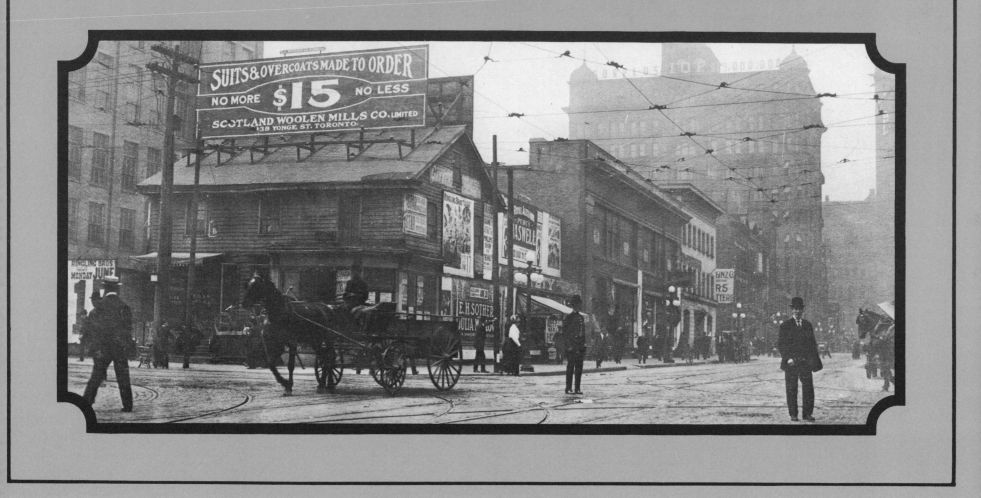

The Toronto Police have the reputation of being a most efficient and zealous force. They have to carry out tasks severe and dangerous, and are on duty for long hours in the arctic winter or tropical summer, at very insufficient pay. The police deserve the sympathy and support of all good citizens.

from C.P. Mulvany, *Toronto Past and Present*, 1885.

To serve and protect is the motto of this brave Toronto policeman directing the busy downtown traffic comprised of horses, wagons, bicycles, cars, cats, dogs and jaywalkers.

The annual police report for 1896 relates that the cases of highway robbery were the same as last year but pocket picking was on the increase. Seventy-five of the 100 instances reported occurred in shops, markets and churches.

The northwest corner of Bay and Adelaide Streets, c.1910.

The building in these pictures housed the Wellington Hotel, the Dominion Telegraph Office and Weller's Stage Coach Lines. The pie-shaped block on which it stood was called the Coffin Block and the western end, or foot, was Scott Street. Wellington and Front Streets formed the sides, tapering together at Church Street.

From this point, radiate the business streets, whose massive warehouses may be seen on every hand. Each firm seems to vie with its neighbour in the erection of elegant and commodious premises with the best facilities for doing business.

from G.M. Adam, *Toronto Old and New*, 1891.

The development of Front and Wellington Streets, c.1872. (above)

Front and Wellington Streets, c.1888. (below)

12

The name of Gooderham has long been linked to the area of Front and Wellington Streets and to the Flat-Iron Building. In 1832, William Gooderham arrived from England, and with his brother-in-law James Worts formed the lucrative distillery Gooderham & Worts. Gooderham who soon became one of the best-known and least-loved capitalists of his day was knighted. He died in 1881 and in 1892 the Gooderham company built its new, elegant headquarters on the Coffin Block. In the 1890's, Flat-Iron Buildings were appearing on pie-shaped lots in major North American cities. The wind tunnel created by New York's Flat-Iron Building at Broadway, Fifth Avenue and 23rd Street prompted the expression *Twenty-three Skidoo*. It seems the wind was always lifting women's skirts and the police were always *shooing* the voyeurs away.

The Flat-Iron, or Gooderham Building, at the corner of Front and Wellington Streets, 1897.

13

Behind the grand arch built in honour of Queen Victoria's jubilee celebration, is Toronto's second City Hall. When it opened in 1899, it was the second largest city hall in North America, exceeded only by the one in Philadelphia. The clock tower, rising 285 feet above the ground, weighs thirteen tons. The clock, with its three bells and twenty foot diameter, takes three hours to wind and uses whale oil to keep its gears moving in sub-zero weather. Of the four gargoyles below the clock, there is only one clearly distinguishable human face—that of architect Edward James Lennox. Because the city fathers refused to commemorate a plaque honouring him, Lennox signed his name and the date under the eaves above all the faces.

Bay Street, with the second City Hall in the background, 1899.

In 1895, Oronhyatekha, supreme chief of the Independent Order of Foresters, wanted nothing but the best for his organization's headquarters and chose brother George Bouinlock to design their Temple Building. This twelve-story sensation, the tallest in the British Empire, had the best heating and air conditioning systems, taps spouting iced water from marble fountains, mosaic walls and floors, doors with embossed copper inlays, pillars of brass and marble, gold leaf ceilings, and special fire-proofing. When the building was demolished in 1971, it was so well-constructed that it had to be dismantled piece by piece.

Bay and Richmond Streets, looking north to the second City Hall, 1907.

15

In 1845, Toronto's 20,000 citizens were most impressed with their first *new* City Hall.

In 1884, the salaries of the city officials ranged from $2,000 per year for the Mayor up to $3,500 for the City Treasurer, down to $1,500 for the Medical Health Officer. The municipal government was carried on by aldermen acting as a committee under the Mayor. These aldermen were unsalaried.

By 1898, the 24 aldermen, elected annually, received $300 per year. The Mayor's salary had been inflated to $3,000 per year and, as an act of grace, he was permitted to have a second and sometimes third term of office.

On the second floor were the offices of the Mayor and city officials. The basement housed cells for prisoners.

Toronto's very first City Hall was situated on the south side of Front Street between Jarvis Street and west of Market Street from 1845-1898.

Behind the trees on the left of this photograph is the Ladies' Seminary of the Bishop Strachan School. Further down the street is the Canada Coffin Company.

The College Avenue Gates, Yonge Street entrance, 1875.

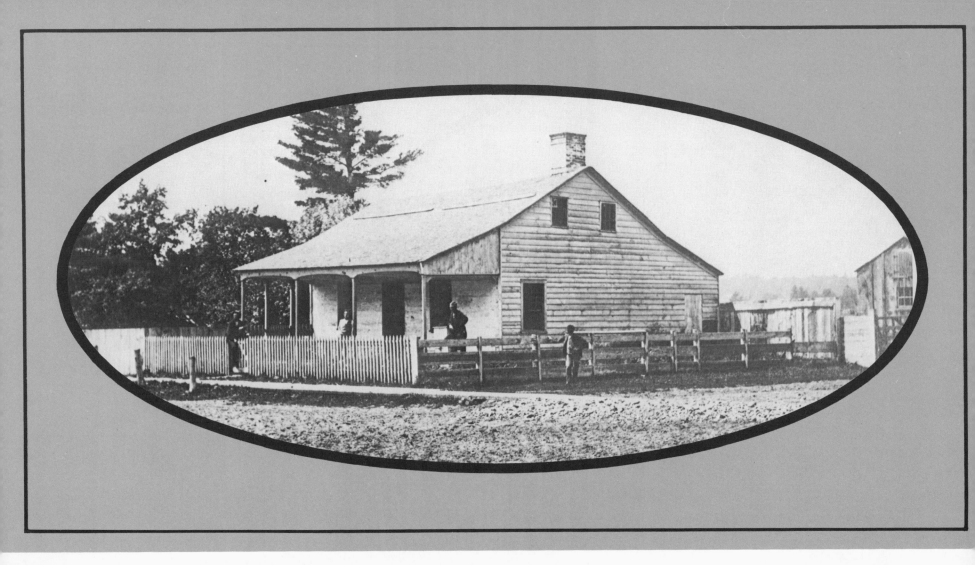

Where the elegant Park Plaza Hotel now stands, there was once a little, one-storey log cabin known as the Tecumseh Wigwam. Built in 1820, it continued to be a popular drinking establishment until 1864. Especially on Sundays, the Wigwam was a favourite resort for young men of elevated social tastes and habits. In the 1850's, it was maintained by an old man named King, whose son George was a member of the notorious band of robbers known as the Townsend Gang. Son George was convicted for the murder of a stage coach driver and hanged at Cayuga.

The Tecumseh Wigwam stood at the northwest corner of Bloor Street and Avenue Road from 1850-1874.

Just north of the Bloor Street toll gate stood the Red Lion Inn, a roomy, two-storey, white, roughcast establishment with a swinging lion rampart sign. Built circa 1810, the inn brought cheer and hospitality to generations of pioneers and batallions of officers who had fought under Wellington at Waterloo. For over 80 years, it served the best strong beer at eight pence a gallon New York currency if drunk in the house, and six pence New York currency if taken out. The Red Lion was not only a substantial, popular place of business, but it also had 200 acres of surrounding land. In 1812, the owner could not get $400 for the whole outfit.

The Red Lion Inn, on the east side of Yonge Street north of Bloor Street, c.1875.

When York became the City of Toronto in 1834, the land stretching to Bloor Street and Yorkville was complete forest with only a few residences. The Yorkville Town Hall was a quaint, picturesque building. Horsecars once passed through its arches and stables stood in the rear yard. Its crest, sculptured in stone and set over the circular window in the front gable, consisted of a beer barrel, anvil, jackplane, brick mould and sheep's head, each with an initial imposed upon it. These were symbols representing the trades and names of the five York councillors at the time it was built. Over the entire crest was a Canadian beaver. The Yorkville Town Hall, completed in 1860 was . . . Toronto's first temperance hall.

Yorkville Town Hall on the west side of Yonge Street opposite Collier Street, 1875.

Today's fashionable Bloor Street was named after the tavern-keeper Joseph Bloor who came from England and later owned a brewery in Yorkville. He was also a benefactor of the Bloor Street Methodist Church.

Yorkville is a popular place of residence for those desiring a somewhat cheaper place of abode. Every morning streetcars run from the Yorkville Town Hall to King Street crowded with businessmen, merchants, clerks and employees. Raised on a hill overlooking the bay, Yorkville is a healthy and economical location; its quiet streets and well-shaped avenues afford pleasant relief after the heat and dust of the city streets in summer.

from C.P. Mulvany, *Toronto Past and Present*, 1884.

A streetsign at the northwest corner of Bloor Street and Avenue Road, 1908. (above)

The four corners of Bloor Street and Avenue Road, c.1900. (below)

21

The Pioneer Hotel, built in the 1850's, was a popular place for farmers with produce. Although tavern regulations were strict regarding "drinking or tippling", the liquor laws were "more honoured in the breach than the observance". Owner Robert Irving was no exception to this rule because it was rumoured that he had "a good local and improving business".

In 1899, the Queen's Hotel on Front Street West, which later became the Royal York Hotel, charged $3 - $4 per night, while the Walker House at Front and York Streets cost $2 - $2.50. Taxi cabs were $1 per hour. For the comfort of weary travellers, some of Toronto's better hotels sent stage coaches adorned with red plush seats to meet their guests as they arrived at the train station.

On the northwest corner of Bloor and Bathurst Streets stood the Pioneer Hotel, c.1890.

Those who planned the city certainly planned for the future. The streets have better ventilation, better drainage and are vastly superior to the hideous jumble of streets and crooked alleys found in such old cities as Montreal and Quebec. The Toronto streets are all wide and all give plenty of room for street traffic. There is plenty of water, plenty of air, plenty of room everywhere and there is plenty of energy in the businessmen of today.

from *The Toronto Mail*, 1893: price 3¢.

Railway crossing at Bloor Street West and Dundas Street, c.1894.

In the early 1900's, parking spots were obviously hard to find — especially if you were driving a horse and sleigh loaded with grain, flour, coal or groceries. But in the 1870's, the village of Little York was mere farmland and the Danforth road was mud and gravel with bush and creeks along the way. The owner of the Charles Gates' Hotel on the north side of Danforth near Main, which later became the Owen's Hotel, had a mile-long race course at the rear of the hotel. Here, the enterprising turfman Seagram of Waterloo stabled and trained his horses. The village was also a popular rendezvous spot for dancing, cycling and sleighing parties. The hotels were always packed with Torontonians on wild weekend sprees.

The inhabitants of the village of Little York, photographed from the Empringham Hotel on the south side of Danforth Avenue west of Dawes Road, 1900.

24

University Avenue has a peculiar history which nothing but the whims of 150 years ago can explain. The avenue was originally designed to be constructed on two roadways. That on the west, begun in 1825, was known as College Street, a pretty avenue, cut through farmland and lined with chestnut trees. In 1842, Park Lane, named after the London thoroughfare, was constructed to the east of College Street and was also lined with attractive trees. The two streets were divided by a high board fence. At the Queen Street entrances to the streets were stout wooden gates, flanked by quaint lodges for the gatekeepers. Later, the two roadways were joined into one, with a boulevard and trees adorning the centre roadway. The gatehouses were replaced with Osgoode Hall on one side and the Canada Life Building on the other.

University Avenue showing the College Avenue Gates, c.1868.

25

On April 9, 1893, Gladys Marie Smith was born at 211 University Avenue. She adopted her great-grandmother's name and, by the time she was 26, had received international recognition and founded the United Artists Studios along with Charlie Chaplin, Douglas Fairbanks and D.W. Griffith. She was . . . Toronto's own . . . Mary Pickford.

University Avenue extends from Queen Street to Queen's Park and is, even to one who has seen the best park drives in Europe and America, from St. James Park in London to the famous Coconut-Palm Avenue at Rio de Janeiro, one of the very finest in the world. In summer when the chestnuts are in blossom, a walk up this avenue is one of the pleasures which Toronto has to offer to her guests.

from C.P. Mulvany, *Toronto Past and Present*, 1884.

University Avenue, 1908.

Ontario's first Parliament Buildings, dating back to 1796, once stood at the corner of Front and Berkeley Streets. After they were burned to the ground by American attackers during the War of 1812, a new brick building was erected at the same site in 1818. That building also burned to the ground. The third Parliament Buildings, shown in this photograph, were built on Front Street, west of the present Union Station. That elaborate building served as the seat of government until April 4, 1893 when the Ontario Legislature opened its 26th session under Premier Sir Oliver Mowat at the new Parliament Buildings situated in Queen's Park at the top of University Avenue.

Ontario's third Parliament Buildings on Front Street, 1884.

It was proposed to employ a band to play in Queen's Park every Sunday afternoon, but this idea was voted down in council, though I confess I see no possible objection to it, except that it would be a welcome diversion to the working man. But it would also be a source of attraction to children who are otherwise penned up in a stifling Sunday School, having dry as dust texts sweltered into their little bodies.

from C.S. Clark, *Of Toronto The Good*, 1898.

In 1860, picturesque Queen's Park was officially opened by the Prince of Wales (later Edward VII). As the gossip goes, he was a most charming fellow, well-known for setting many a maidenly heart aflutter.

The Legislative Building of Ontario, Parliament Buildings, situated in Queen's Park, 1900.

When Queen Victoria died in 1901, she was succeeded by her son Edward VII (Prince of Wales) who, in 1860, had made the first Royal Visit to Toronto. Edward VII immediately sent his son and daughter-in-law, the Duke and Duchess of Cornwall and York, off to Canada on an imperial cruise. They arrived in Toronto in October, 1901. Anxious to extend a true royal welcome, the Toronto manufacturers raised $10,000 to build a triumphal arch made of stucco. Not to be upstaged, The Independent Order of Foresters also built a glorious arch at Bay and Richmond Streets. The downtown merchants set the city ablaze with flags, decorations and the extravagant use of electric lights.

Toronto Manufacturers' Arch, located at the entranceway to Queen's Park north of College Street, built for the Duke and Duchess of Cornwall and York, 1901.

29

It's hard to believe but there was once a stream of water that flowed across trendy Bloor Street into the University of Toronto campus. The stream, affectionately called Old Taddle or Taddle Creek ended at McCaul's Pond. Here, many a freshman was treated to a watery initiation and many a Torontonian brought a beloved dog for a Sunday scrub.

McCaul's Pond on the campus of the University of Toronto which later became part of the Hart House complex, c.1880.

The magnificent University College building, the mother house of the University of Toronto, was built in 1856. Today, it is still considered one of the finest examples of Norman architecture on the continent. In 1890, fire destroyed 35,000 books and valuable documents here, but the walls of the University College building remained miraculously intact.

The University College building, University of Toronto, c.1885.

The Belt Line streetcar ran down Spadina Avenue, along King Street, up Sherbourne Street and along the Bloor Street tracks. Because the ride encircled the major part of Toronto, it offered residents and visitors an opportunity to view splendid stores on King Street, exquisite suburban residences, squalid downtown shanties, fashionable hotels and the city's great educational institutions. Taking the Belt Line trip was a most popular and economical activity, and on a balmy summer evening, the cars were crowded with families out for an airing. Doctors even prescribed this trip as a refreshing bedtime stimulant and diversion.

The Belt Line streetcar at the corner of Spadina Avenue and College Street, c.1893.

At the turn of the century, it was possible for a thirsty man, horse and dog to take a drink at the same place, at the same time, from a public water trough. These cast iron troughs were located at strategic points throughout the city. Some were round in shape and designed only for horses. Others, such as the one in this photograph, had a brass drinking cup chained to the upper portion on the sidewalk side of the trough which allowed humans to get refreshed while their beloved pets drank from the basin at the bottom.

The memorable water trough in the College Street and Spadina Avenue area, 1899.

33

In 1830, after the ambitious lawyer Dr. William Warren Baldwin had acquired great amounts of land and wealth, he built a mansion called Spadina House on the edge of a hill near the present-day Casa Loma. His grand dream was to found a feudal estate where a Baldwin of Spadina would always live. From Spadina to the highway leading into town, Dr. Baldwin cut a wide, magnificent road lined with chestnut trees. That road is the Spadina Avenue of today. Ironically, when Baldwin's son Robert became a leader of the Liberal Party, he passed a bill abolishing the inheritance of a family estate by the eldest son and dissolved forever his father's feudal fantasies.

Spadina Avenue looking north from Queen Street, 1907.

Jarvis Street is lined on either side by the mansions of the upper ten. Of a summer morning, it is pleasant to saunter down the street while the chestnut trees are fresh with the life of June, and the bunches of blossom are as beautiful as any of the exotic flowers in the gardens of the houses.

from C.P. Mulvany, *Toronto Past and Present*, 1884.

Take a walk through the residential parts of Toronto and look at the mile upon mile of solid brick and stone houses. Then compare these with the gaudy, painted wooden shells upon the residential streets of Buffalo or Detroit and wonder why people in the United States live in wooden cottages such as our citizens occupy in the summer at the Island.

from *The Toronto Mail*, 1893: price 3¢.

Jarvis Street looking south towards Carlton Street, 1888. (above)

Jarvis Street, c. 1905. (below)

Rosedale is a beautifully situated suburb on the far side of the picturesque ravine north of the eastern part of Bloor Street, with magnificent bridges at either end spanning the ravine. The banks of the beautiful glen, rich with the loveliest colours of the spring seem *for talking age and whispering lovers made*. Rosedale is the name given to the homestead of the aristocratic family of Jarvis.

Rosedale House was the scene of many a festive gathering of the chief and ladies of the Family Compact, a political and social clique who were the most polished and cultured society of their day. The suburb takes its name from the abundant rose-growths in the gardens of its numerous mansions and villas.

from C.P. Mulvany, *Toronto Past and Present*, 1884.

Rosedale Ravine Drive, with the Sherbourne Street bridge in the background, 1897.

There is one spot in the vicinity of *Muddy York* which all visitors to the Queen City should make a point of visiting. The valley of the Don, a winding stream that flows on the east of the city, offers the prettiest bit of landscape in the neighborhood.

from *Canadian Illustrated News*, 1871.

Turkey shooting on the Don is an annual *fête* among our Toronto sportsmen. The tournament is held on the Don River and is attended partly for sport and for the chance of procuring a Christmas dinner for twenty-five cents.

from *Canadian Illustrated News*, 1876.

Skinny dipping in the Don River near the Bloor Street viaduct, 1910.

It was in the year 1883 that Toronto became land hungry and began to stretch forth ambitious hands to seize adjoining sections of the county of York. Real estate men and companies began to open large tracts of land and farms became converted into building lots. Up to this date, Bloor Street on the north, Dufferin Street on the west and the Don River on the east marked the boundaries of our city whose area was 6,771 acres. In 1883, Yorkville threw in its lot with the Queen City.

from C.S. Clark, *Of Toronto The Good*, 1898.

Bathurst and Davenport Streets, looking south to Bathurst Street. On the right is the Hillcrest Race Track, c.1908.

In 1890, Toronto discovered that she had grown even too strong and that she had acquired enough territory to hold all the citizens we are likely to have for the next fifty years.

from C.S. Clark, *Of Toronto The Good*, 1898.

Bathurst Street north of St. Clair Avenue, c.1907.

Hand in hand with this tremendous extension of territory went local improvements and the increase of our debenture debt. For the past six years, our citizens have been wondering what all the territory was ever wanted for and have been cursing the insane speculative mania which sewered, paved and sidewalked the grassy fields of the county of York.

from C.S. Clark, *Of Toronto The Good*, 1898.

Walking the plank on St. Clair Avenue, c.1909.

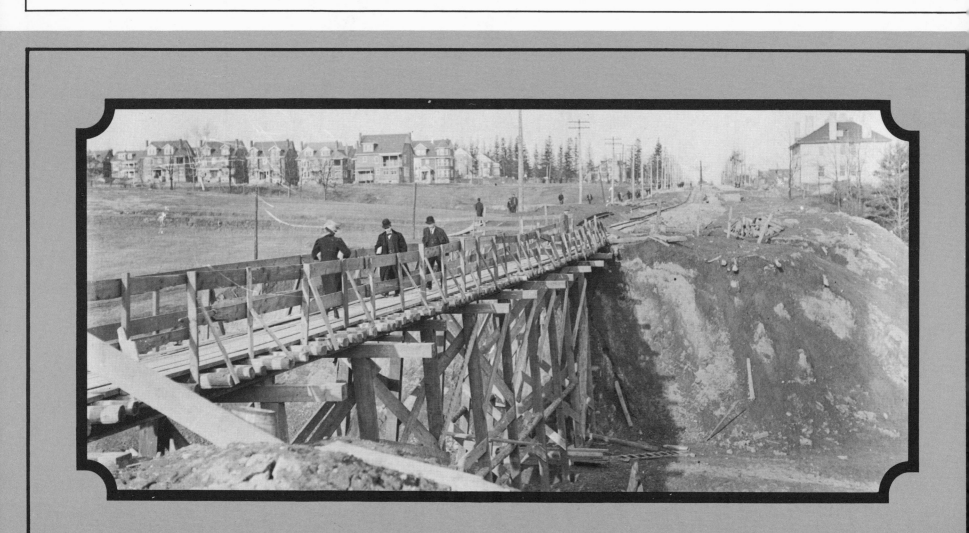

For Sale:
Yonge Street from St. Clair Avenue to Yonge Boulevard.

If only I had known . . .

During the seven fat years from 1883-1890, when Toronto's sober population became land-crazy and speculation-mad, it is really comical to note some of the ideas people began to have regarding the value of their land. To trace this matter up, I wrote to a firm of real estate agents in reference to a house on Charles Street. It was not by any means a new house, but it was rented for sixteen dollars a month and taxes. Buying price: 3,200 dollars! This is not by any means an exceptional case. I could give you similar ones by the score.

from C.S. Clark, *Of Toronto The Good*, 1898.

The northeast corner of Yonge Street and Eglinton Avenue, c.1905.

In the dress of ladies, great latitude is allowed; but the aim of the gentle sex should be simplicity and taste. The street dress of a lady should be simple and without display. To dress conspicuously or in brilliant colours for the street is a sign of bad breeding. In bad weather, a light India-rubber waterproof with a hood is more convenient and better protection than an umbrella. To wear much jewelry on the street is vulgar. In large cities, it subjects a lady to the danger of robbery or to conspicuous notice. Modesty in dress and behaviour add more charm to a woman than the rustle of silk or the glitter of gold.

from G. Nichols, *The Great Nineteenth Century Household Guide*, 1894.

Ladies out for a stroll, Eglinton Avenue near Bathurst Street, c.1910.

42

The farmer has the most health-ful employment. He has an abundance of pure air and is usu-ally not necessitated to expose himself to storm and rain. His regular habits and labour in the open air give him a good appe-tite, digestion, and capacity for sleep. His brain is not worried or overtaxed. Some of the disad-vantages of farmer life are poorly ventilated bedrooms, over-heated rooms in winter, eating too much and the use of tea, coffee and tobacco. Aside from these abuses, the farmer's life, more than any other, tends to longevity. Don't be in a hurry, young man, to leave the farm. You may live to regret the day of your leaving it.

from G. Nichols, *The Great Nineteenth Century Medicine Manual*, 1894.

A farm in the Yonge Street and Eglinton Avenue area, 1909. (above)

A farm on the northwest corner of Yonge Street and Lawrence Avenue, c.1895. (below)

43

This general store, owned and operated by Mr. J.J. Davis also housed the Davisville Post Office from 1894-1913. The store later became known as the Curiosity Shop.

Had there not been added thousands of acres of goose pastures, we should now have a compact city, light taxation, and a better and more prosperous population.

from C.S. Clark, *Of Toronto The Good*, 1898.

The northeast corner of Yonge Street and Davisville Avenue, 1900.

York Mills, c.1909.

Don't jump! Buy!

In the 1850's, the Hoggs brothers bought and opened a subdivision at York Mills which became known as Hogg's Hollow. From 1804 to 1926, there were three mill sites located in York Mills and the sound of water running over waterwheels, the buzz of saws cutting logs and the noise of stones grinding the grains were heard throughout the valley everyday. The landscape was dotted with houses, out-houses, blacksmiths' shops and a thriving tavern on north Yonge Street.

The district known as Jefferson derived its name from the family of William Thomas Jefferson who settled on Lot 59, Concession 1, Vaughan Township in 1857. The Jefferson General Store and Post Office was established in 1882 and remained in operation until 1968.

In 1890, there were 182 letter carriers, 191 street letterboxes, but only 12 street letterbox collectors. In the pre-airmail days of 1910, the cost of delivering a letter anywhere in Canada was all of 1¢. After 1915, the cost of delivery was doubled to 2¢. The length of time for mail delivery? . . . same as today, anybody's guess.

The Jefferson Post Office, Yonge Street north of Richmond Hill, c.1910.

2

Where
we worked

The occupations listed in the Toronto census of 1871 reveal there were 2,872 servants, 2,184 common labourers, 1,413 clerks, 1,100 carpenters, 36 saddlers, 48 brewers and distillers, 302 hotelkeepers, 683 shoemakers and 232 blacksmiths.

In the field of crafts and culture, there were 70 booksellers, 381 printers and publishers, 56 carvers and gilders, 41 photographers, 40 engravers and 31 architects. In a new category listed in 1891, there were 78 artists and literateurs. Toward the top of the social pyramid were 109 clergy, 96 physicians, 206 lawyers, 20 bankers, 183 gentlemen . . . and the grand total of 108 government employees!

In 1907, permits were issued to 817 peddlars, 508 rag collectors and 60 junk dealers. Many others worked illegally because they didn't have the money to buy the permit.

Work crew paving the roads at Bathurst Street and Davenport Road, c.1910.

Toronto's building boom in the early 1900's provided much work for immigrants. With the money they earned paving roads and building sewers they were able to settle in the city and then send for their families in Europe. These immigrants lived in squalid homes with cesspools, outhouses and insufficient heating. They worked under dangerous conditions constructing Toronto's sewer system, enduring long hours and always risking the effects of noxious gases and sudden cave-ins.

Early records show that underground sewers were in existence in Toronto in 1840 and that modern toilet facilities came into general use in 1880.

Building sewers at Garrison Creek, 1899. (above)

Building the Marion Street sewer, 1912. (below)

Among the most important public buildings of recent date must be classed the Arcade between Yonge and Victoria Streets. With its front entrance on Yonge Street, the beauty of its imposing cut-stone facade with its wide archway and pillars is a valuable addition. The spacious passageway of the Arcade is furnished with stalls, glittering with all that is most attractive to pleasure-seekers. The Arcade will be to our city what the Burlington Arcade is to London, the Palais Royal to Paris, the haunt of fashionable loungers, the bazaar where visitors to Toronto carry away some momento of their stay, a most commendable commercial speculation for whose success we must all wish.

from C.P. Mulvany, *Toronto Past and Present*, 1884.

The interior of the Yonge Street Arcade on the east side of Yonge opposite Temperance Street, c.1895. (above)

The exterior of the Yonge Street Arcade, c.1885. (below)

Construction of the very first streetcar tracks on Yonge Street from Yorkville to the heart of the city took about three weeks. Finally, on a September afternoon in 1861, the very first horsecar rolled down the street, accompanied by the musical strains of an artillery bank playing on the roof. Unfortunately, this maiden voyage was delayed twice by derailments. People treated this modern innovation with great enthusiasm and remained in good spirits in spite of all delays. As they had done with stage coach travel, passengers were always willing to give a push, shove and lift to get the new horsecars moving again.

Constructing the streetcar tracks at Roncesvalles Avenue at Queen and King Streets, 1910.

POSITI
>NO<
SMOKING
BY ORDER
STREET COM[

The Western City Yard was one of several yards around Toronto where horse-drawn carts and wheels were made for use by the City Engineer's Department.

Machinists, and all whose occupation exposes them to an atmosphere loaded with dust, are liable to irritation and inflammation of the respiratory organs, resulting in asthma or consumption. Blacksmiths are exposed to dust and the intense light of the fire often injures the eyes.

from G. Nichols, *The Great Nineteenth Century Medicine Manual*, 1894.

Western City Yard, 1116 King Street West, c.1896.

There seems to be a general impression that a continued meat diet is absolutely essential and with some, it seems unwise to omit meat for a single meal. There is no civilized country in the world in which so much meat is eaten or in which so much is wasted by bad cooking and absolute unthrift. We all eat too much meat, too much for our health and too much for our pocketbooks. Great, brawny Scotchmen live month after month on oatmeal and buttermilk, and a healthier, harder working class of men it would be difficult to find. Our general health would be greatly improved if our diet were to consist more of vegetables, grains and fruit.

from G. Nichols, *The Great Nineteenth Century Household Guide*, 1894.

On the northwest corner of Carlton and Parliament Streets was the Joseph W. Weston butcher shop, c.1896.

No matter how large the establishment, no person plays a more important part than the cook. With her rests not only the comfort, but the health of those she serves. A dirty kitchen is a disgrace, and cleanliness is a most essential ingredient in the art of cooking. When at work, dress suitably. Wear short, plain gowns, well-fitting boots and large aprons with bibs.

Golden Rules for the Kitchen:
1. Without cleanliness and punctuality good cooking is impossible.
2. Clean and clear as you go.
3. A time for everything and everything in time.
4. A good cook wastes nothing.
5. An hour lost in the morning has to be run after all day.
6. Haste without hurry saves worry, fuss and flurry.

from G. Nichols, *The Great Nineteenth Century Household Guide*, 1894.

The Wm. Davies grocery store on Queen Street West near Bay Street in City Hall Square, c.1905.

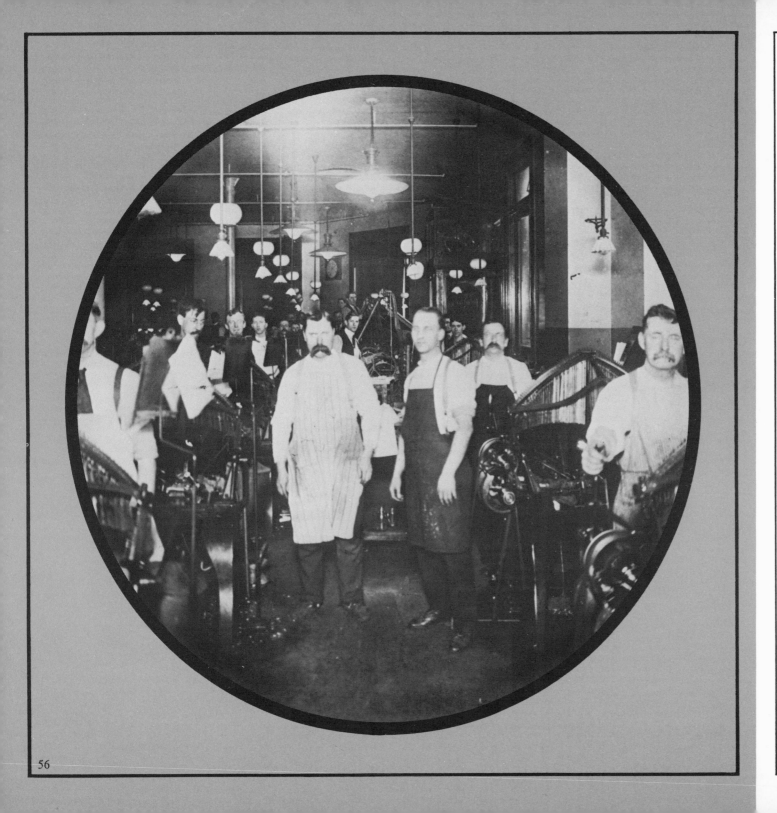

The Evening Telegram was born on April 17, 1876. During its first year, it was a 2¢ paper with limited circulation. In 1877, it was changed to a 1¢ paper with five editions daily.

Mr. J. Ross Robertson, publisher and proprietor, has broken the long monopoly of the expensive and cumbrous party papers by the establishment and successful management of this live city evening newspaper. No more long sermon-like editorials, but leading articles on the topics of the day from a commonsense standpoint. The Telegram is an institution in Toronto read by everyone from the fashionable belle in her boudoir to Biddy in the basement!

from C.P. Mulvany, Toronto Past and Present, 1884.

The interior of the composing room of The Evening Telegram (later The Toronto Telegram), 57 Yonge Street near King Street, c.1904.

The Evening Telegram, the pioneer of independent press in Canada, is par excellence the family newspaper of the city. When the day's toil is over, when the bread winners of the household, father, mother and girls have been emancipated by the welcome six o'clock bell, when the supper has been partaken of, what is more welcome than the old familiar *Telegram? The Telegram* has a circulation of about 15,500 daily and its success has been phenomenal. It is claimed, and we believe justly, that it has been a paying concern since the day it was first issued.

from C.P. Mulvany, *Toronto Past and Present,* 1884.

On October 31, 1971, *The Toronto Telegram* ceased publication due to financial difficulties.

The interior of the press room of The Evening Telegram (*later* The Toronto Telegram), *57 Yonge Street near King Street, 1905.*

The very first Weston bread factory was located at the rear of Sullivan Street opposite Grange Place. Later, Mr. Weston built a larger bread plant at Soho Square and Phoebe Street which he sold to Canada Bread. At the end of a ten-year contract in which he agreed to stay out of the bread business, he built another factory on Bathurst Street opposite the Western Hospital. When he sold this plant, he moved his lucrative business to Dupont Street. When it was taken over by Canada Bread, he began manufacturing biscuits and cookies and built yet another factory on Peter Street. In the right foreground of this photograph are Mr. and Mrs. George Weston, with their baking and delivery staff, in front of their very first bread factory.

The first George Weston bread factory, c. 1895.

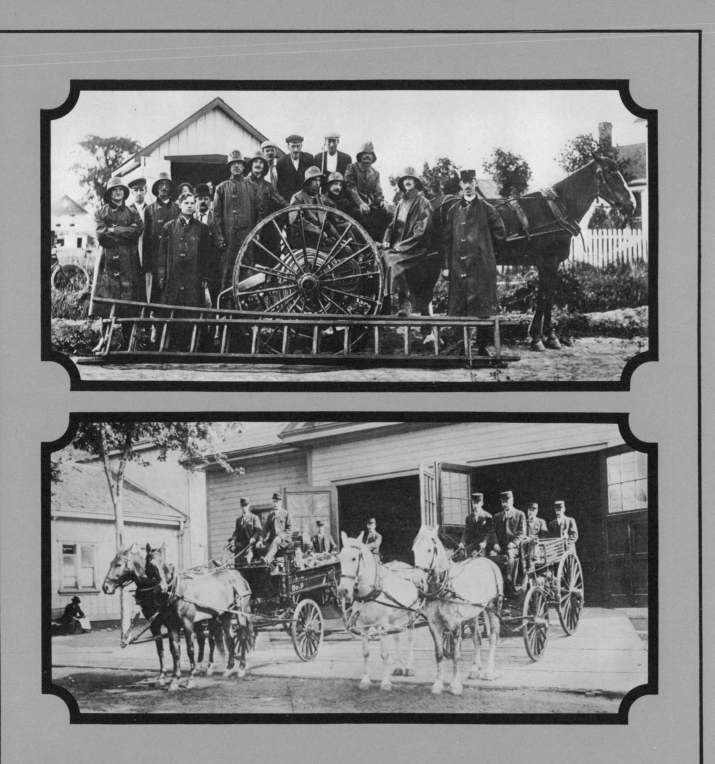

In 1820, a law was passed in Toronto, then called the Town of York, which required that every householder keep two leather buckets hanging in front of his house. When the fire alarm was rung from the bell at the church, citizens would form a bucket brigade to the nearest waterhole to fight the fire. In 1874, the Toronto Fire Department was instituted with a force consisting of 36 men. Before this time, firefighters were volunteers. Because Toronto experienced such rapid growth between 1883 and 1912, the number of fire stations increased from eight to twenty-seven to ensure that all parts of the city would have adequate fire protection.

The Bedford Park Volunteer Fire Brigade, c.1905. (above)

The old firehall at the Canadian National Exhibition, 1906. (below)

59

By 1900, working outside the home had become a necessity for many struggling Toronto women, especially immigrants. In 1891, of the 164 occupations listed, 87 employed more than one woman. In 1898, Ontario factory inspector Margaret Carlyle marvelled at the versatility of the women who worked in 120 different areas of employment, including spring and woolen factories.

The 1889 Annual Report of the Ontario Bureau of Industries states that "female workers over sixteen years of age without dependents earned $216.71 per year, and with the cost of living at $214.28, had a surplus of $2.43. Female workers over sixteen years of age with dependents earned $300.13 per year, including the earnings of their dependents. These females had a deficit of $14.23".

Women and men working at the looms in the woolen factory, 1908.

In 1885 Robert Simpson installed two telephones and began his large, busy mail order service. If you wanted to make a purchase from Simpson's 1896 mail order office, here were some invaluable items at unbeatable prices: Women's kid button boots, $1.00. Wool blankets, $2.10. 36" Factory cotton, 4¢ per yard. Children's eiderdown coats with fur trimming, $1.50. Greenland seal capes, $18.00. Opossum muffs, $2.00. And their famous mail order slogan went something like this . . .

"Through our mail order system, we are enabled to serve the needs of shoppers in the farthermost sections of the Dominion. No department of this great business is better organized. None gives more perfect satisfaction. The same individual care that is given to the shopper standing in front of our counter is given to orders to reach us by mail".

The mail order office of the Robert Simpson Company Limited, 1910.

Alexander Graham Bell established Toronto's first telephone exchange in March of 1879 with the grand total of 40 subscribers. At that time, telephone service rang from the Toronto Telephone Dispatch Company, situated at 10 King Street East. It was their company policy to hire only male operators.

In the early 1900's, working as a telephone operator for *Ma Bell* was a job that a girl of the better class could accept.

The Bell Telephone Company officially changed its name to Bell Canada in 1968.

The Bell Telephone Company head office, c.1909.

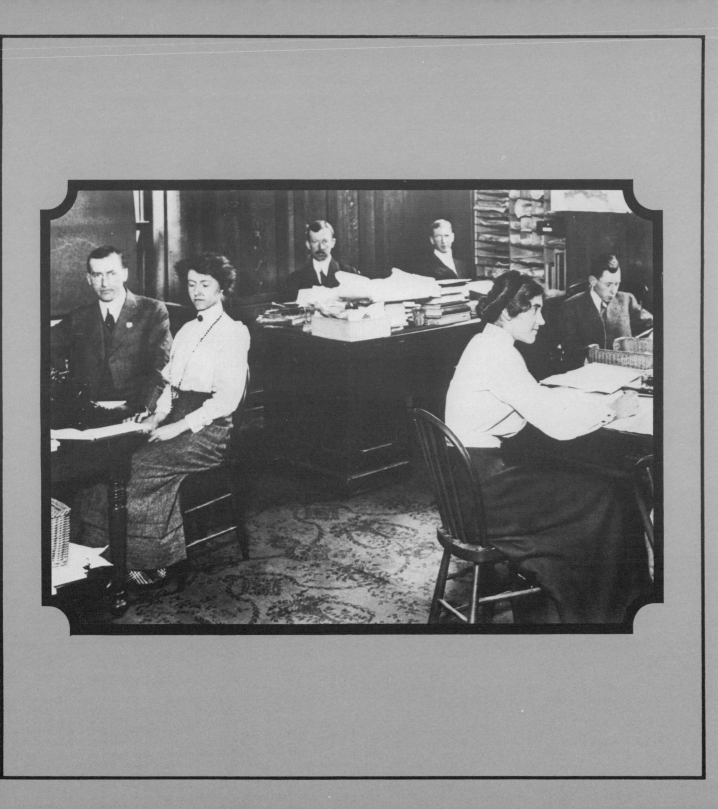

In the 1900's, education was obviously no laughing matter.

The existing public school system is the work of one man of good sense, the late Rev. Egerton Ryerson, who modelled, remodelled and established it on its present firm basis. Dr. Ryerson travelled extensively, at government expense, in the United States, England and Europe to study educational methods. The public schools of Toronto are built on modifications of Italian renaissance and have lofty classrooms, wide corridors and ample accommodation for playgrounds. The average salaries of public school teachers are, of males $720, of females $324. It is much to be desired that this shall be considerably raised.

from C.P. Mulvany, *Toronto Past and Present*, 1884.

The Ministry Office of the Board of Education at the Normal School, located at the site of today's Ryerson Polytechnical Institute, 1909.

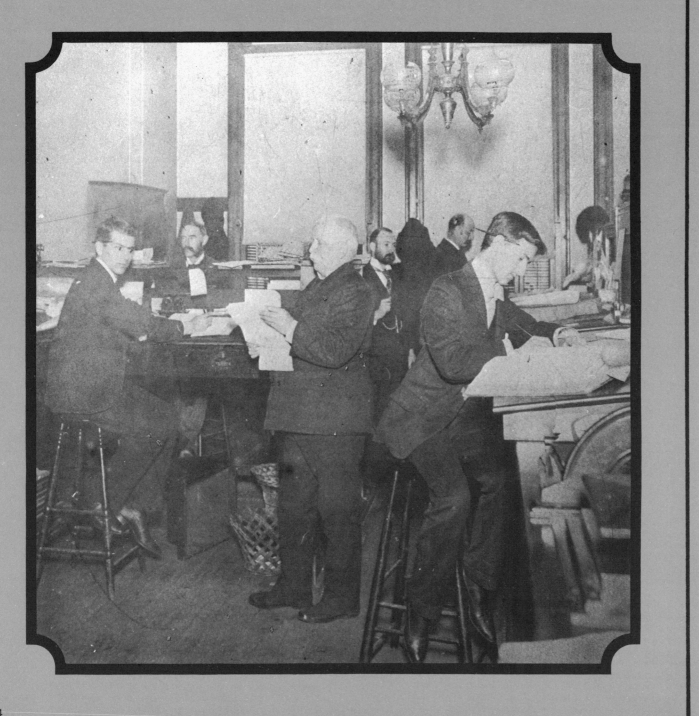

There are several loan companies that do business in savings that must not be overlooked. The loan, savings, and investment companies of the city do a large business and are towers in Toronto's financial strength. They are all very ably managed by capable men, and enjoy perfect security and public confidence.

from *The Toronto Mail,* 1893: price 3¢.

And now about that friendly loan we were talking about . . .

The employees of the Union Loan and Savings Company located on Toronto Street south of Adelaide Street East, 1895.

The poorer classes are to be met with in all parts of the city, but Bathurst Street, Lombard Street and the heart of the city are places where they are the most numerous. The majority of them are, beyond a doubt, honest and willing to work, and in times of great commercial activity can nearly all find employment. But in dull seasons, when merchants and manufacturers are forced to discharge their employees, hundreds are thrown out of employment and the greatest suffering and distress prevail.

from C.S. Clark, *Of Toronto The Good*, 1898.

Rag picker plodding through the snowy streets, c.1910.

65

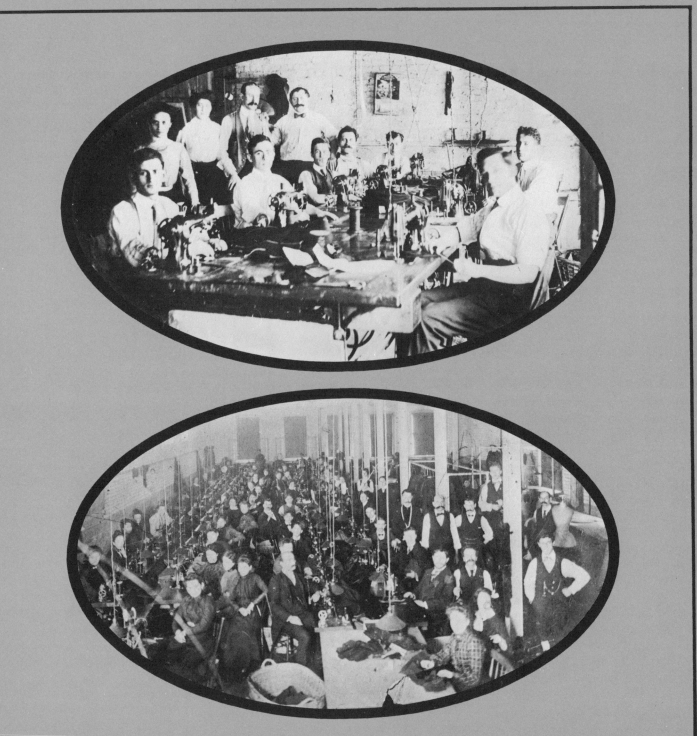

Toronto is a manufacturing city in every sense of the term. Its manufacturers give it the population and energy which it possesses. The average paid each employee is $355.00 per year. This average wage is much larger than that of the United States, which in 1890, was only $309.00 per year. This is also a startling fact for those pessimists who point to the prosperity of the artizan class across the border.

from *The Toronto Mail,* 1893: price 3¢.

At first glance, working indoors at the sewing machine or the presser's iron appeared to be easy in comparison to the difficulties of constant outdoor work. But such was not the case. Factory work was excruciating, with its relentless hours, demanding piece-work quotas, tough foremen, job competition and abysmal ventilation and sanitary conditions.

Women and men working in a typical Toronto sweatshop tailoring factory, c.1895.

But while the visiting merchant sees only the smooth and finished side of the business picture, it is true that there is a dark side to it also. He should see the struggles of the employees to keep themselves in clothing and the necessities of life. He should see them submit to the overbearing manner and petty tyranny of someone who has had the good fortune to get into a position of trust.

from C.S. Clark, *Of Toronto The Good*, 1898.

Our lives shall not be sweated from birth until life closes.
Hearts starve as well as bodies,
Give us bread but give us roses.

from *Garment Workers' Marching Song*, 1908.

Interior of typical Toronto sweatshop tailoring factory, c.1895.

Newspaper advertisements for employment frequently appear when the young man must be a drug clerk, telegraph operator, bookkeeper and goodness knows what else. For example: *Wanted: Hustler to sell ordered clothing and expert at measuring and selling cotton for tweed.*

Wanted: Boy who can write short-hand and caligraph quickly and make himself general useful.
Wanted: Youth to assist in office. Must have bicycle and be anxious for advancement. I would like to hear whether these youths got $2.50, $3 or $4 per week.

Here is one absolutely princely advertisement: *Wanted: Young lady as bookkeeper and cash, $2.50 to $3 per week.*
Was the young lady expected to prostitute herself to obtain money for clothing?

from C.S. Clark, *Of Toronto The Good*, 1898.

Waiting for opportunity to knock, c.1909.

There is nothing in this world so sensitive as the stock market. When a man dabbles in stocks, he needs a pilot as much as a ship entering a rocky channel. Messrs. Cox and Co. are the pilots through whose means many have been guided to safety. Mr. Cox is all activity and bustle. He can tell you in a moment if a stock is going up or down. With him it is a science. Never a point misses him.

from C.P. Mulvany, *Toronto Past and Present*, 1884.

Man's inhumanity to man is not more strikingly exemplified than in the schemes designed to make money out of the credulous. Take my advice. Having to do with the stock exchange. You will be nipped as sure as your name is what it is.

from C.S. Clark, *Of Toronto The Good*, 1898.

Wheeling and dealing at the Standard Stock Exchange, 43 Scott Street at the corner of Wellington Street, 1910.

Today a flagpole,
Tomorrow . . . the CN Tower.

Painters suffer from the action
and from the fumes of the spirits
of turpentine which they con-
stantly inhale. Painters are rarely
advanced in years. They should
be paid double ordinary wages, if
health is to be measured by
money.

from G. Nichols, *The Great Nineteenth Century Medicine Manual*, 1894.

*The flagpole painter on the roof of the
old Custom's House, Front and
Yonge Streets, 1906.*

3

Where
we played

Summertime in the early 1900's and the living was exciting . . .for some.

The parks resounded with brass bands. Boat houses and rowing clubs lined the lake front. Dance pavilions, ice cream parlours and amusement parks were packed with people. The beaches were overflowing with families determined to cool off. And always, around the first of June, the servants of the city's aristocracy began the elaborate preparations necessary to move their masters' households to their elegant summer homes situated at the Toronto Islands, Balmy Beach, Burlington Beach, Long Branch or Oakville. For lovers, there were moonlight excursions on coal burning steamers like the *Chippewa* and the *Cayuga* where they danced on the decks to the strains of *Sweet Adeline*.

Playful bathers posing at Scarborough Beach Park, located in the east end, between McLean and Leuty Avenues south of Queen Street, c.1910.

At a time when there were rules for almost all areas of human behaviour, summertime was no excuse to let appearances down. A gentleman never took off his jacket. A lady wore a summer corset, except in the privacy of her home, where she slipped into something comfortable—a wrapper or tea gown. Respectability was maintained at all times!

The boardwalk at Scarborough Beach Park, 1910. (above)

The popular amusement park at Scarborough Beach Park, 1907. (below)

The great secret in acquiring a bright, beautiful skin is temperance, exercise and cleanliness. High living and late hours will destroy the most beautiful complexion. Those who desire to be beautiful and healthy should never drink strong coffee, nor eat warm bread and butter or fat meat. Moderate diet and frequent bathing will ensure health and beauty. A lady who possesses a beautiful face should preserve it by wearing a veil on going into the open air or sunlight. To powder and paint the cheek of beauty is ridiculous. There is no such beauty as a rosy cheek which nature paints.

from G. Nichols, *The Great Nineteenth Century Household Guide*, 1894.

Sunnyside free bathing beach, c.1908.

The chic ladies of the time were all reading *The Ladies Journal*, the only purely fashion monthly issued in the Dominion.

During its brief existence, *The Ladies Journal* has obtained a circulation of over 42,000 a month which is nothing short of marvellous. It is a paper published entirely in the interests of the ladies, consisting of twenty pages of all that is new and interesting in the fashion world, with illustrations, and the latest in household recipes, domestic matters, short and serial stories of high order, musical selections and much more that is interesting to the ladies. It is well edited, neatly printed and published at the ridiculously low price of 50¢ a year, being the cheapest and best publication in the Dominion.

from C.P. Mulvany, *Toronto Past and Present*, 1884.

The Easter Sunday parade along the Sunnyside Boardwalk, 1909.

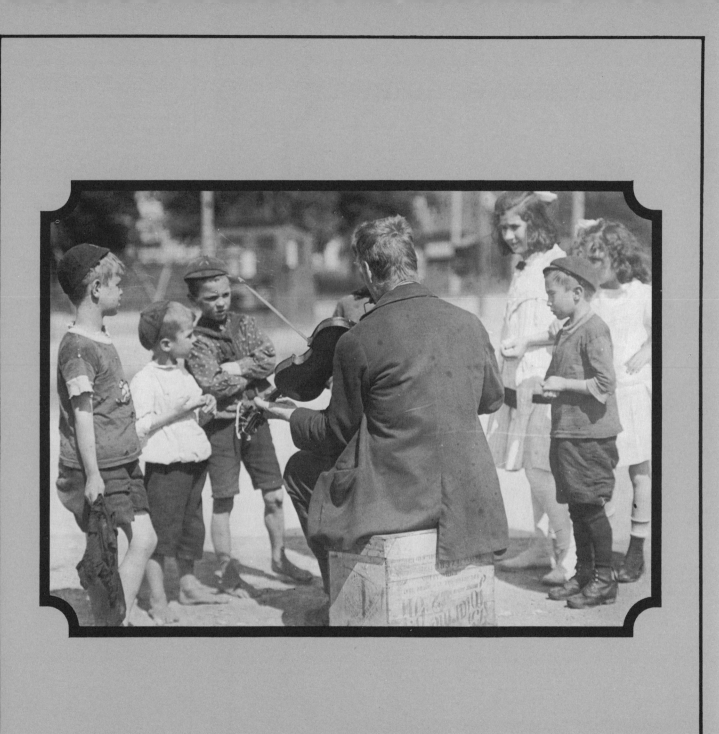

On the subject of music, *The Evening Telegram* comments: "Toronto has a chorus of musical enthusiasts whose alleged desire for high class orchestral entertainment makes more clamour in the papers than their money makes in the box office of Massey Hall."

And on the subject of encores the paper further comments: "Applause, indiscriminate and hearty, crowns every musical performance. Encores are too common. All the orchestras, brass bands, balladists, comic singers and elocutionists are honoured with an enthusiastic recall. When the worst singer is recalled, the encore ceases to be a compliment and becomes a nuisance. Many people are kept away from concerts by the certainty that an encore will follow. Like the rain, the encore falleth up on the just and the unjust."

from C.S. Clark, *Of Toronto The Good*, 1898.

The fiddler at Sunnyside Beach entertaining his enthusiastic young fans, c.1910.

Canada has no general divorce law, but Canadians who desire divorces can get them just as Americans do — in Chicago and other states where they can be obtained. The non-existence of a divorce law is no bar to divorce being obtained. No less a person than Mrs. George E. Foster, wife of the ex-Minister of Finance of Canada, obtained a divorce from her first husband in Chicago. She could not have obtained it in Canada as her first husband is simply a fugitive. What she has done other Canadians can do and will do. Hence a divorce court is not a necessity in Canada.

from C.S. Clark, *Of Toronto The Good*, 1898.

Lovers skiing arm in arm in High Park, c.1910.

At the Social Purity Congress held in Baltimore, Rev. C. M. Watch of Brighton, Ontario congratulated the Canadian people on having no general divorce law. To procure a divorce, he explained, requires a special act of Parliament, and the result is that only 48 applications have been filed in ten years. Forty of these were granted or about one for every 7,000 marriages. The statistical yearbook shows that since 1867, Parliament has had 57 divorces: 40 for Ontario, 14 for Quebec, two for Manitoba, one from the Territories. Divorce courts have been operating in three provinces, with the result that 82 divorces were granted in Nova Scotia, 64 in New Brunswick and 31 in British Columbia.

from C.S. Clark, *Of Toronto The Good*, 1898.

Lovers sitting on the cannon in High Park, 1910.

High Park, situated north of Sunnyside Beach and extending northward about one mile to Bloor Street, is Toronto's great natural park and was a gift of the late John G. Howard. Throughout its 335 acres of hills, valleys and plains, thickly wooded with a great variety of trees, it is a veritable treasure ground of natural beauty gems. Here and there along its winding drives may be seen duck ponds, streams, zoological gardens, playgrounds, flower gardens and in winter, skating rinks, toboggan slides and ski jumps.

from *Diamond Jubilee of Confederation Celebration*, Toronto City Hall Archives Documents, 1917.

Skating in High Park, 1907.

If you wish to be subject to coughs, colds and fevers, shut yourself in close, hot rooms day and night. If you wish to be free from their companionship, always have plenty of pure air to breathe night and day, take daily outdoor exercise, regardless of the weather.

from G. Nichols, *The Great Nineteenth Century Medicine Manual,* 1894.

Snow shoeing in High Park, 1909.

In the spring of 1870, there were so many bicycle accidents that pressure was mounting from injured and worried citizens. When the list of recent victims was presented to the Legislature, it appeared that most of the injured were lawyers. One politician commented, "Well, this proves that the bicycle riders are doing some useful work."

According to an 1895 traffic census, 395 cyclists passed the corners of Yonge and King Streets between 6 and 6:30 p.m. everyday. Toronto had over 90 stores that sold only bicycles which cost around $100 apiece. H.A. Lozier and Company, local bicycle distributors called them "the greatest aid to human locomotion ever devised by mortal hand."

Bicycling in High Park, c.1905.

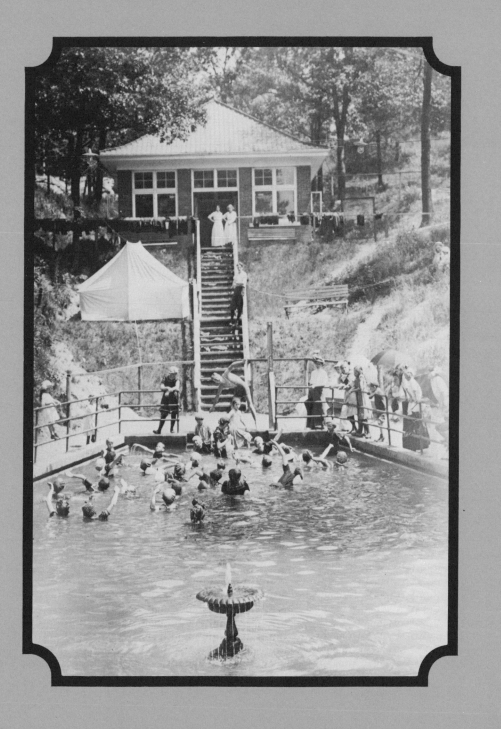

It is impossible to give any rule about bathing which will apply to all persons. Each in this must be a law unto himself. You hear some strong man, who delights in the bracing shock of cold water when he rises from his warm bed advise others to adopt his rule. Again, you will hear a man who resorts to the Turkish bath four times a week urge his friend to follow his example. However, it must be said that everyone can take baths in some form and everyone should. Everyone knows the delicious feeling of cleanliness, the glow of the skin and the robust health which follow a good bath. What is more delightful than the exhilaration of a swim in salt water?

from G. Nichols, *The Great Nineteenth Century Medicine Manual*, 1894.

Mineral baths in High Park, c.1910.

It's hard to believe that Toronto's Old Fort, or Fort York, built with such ambition by Governor John Graves Simcoe, once stood on wooded land surrounded by the lake. In 1793, Simcoe sailed to Toronto Bay from Newark on the H.M. Schooner *Mississauga*. To honour the success of the Duke of York in defeating Napoleon, he ordered a 21-gun salute and named the new fort *York*. Simcoe his wife Elizabeth, their children and staff moved into the famous Canvas House that once belonged to the famed circumnavigator Captain Cook, a friend of Simcoe's father. Elizabeth Simcoe, an energetic 27 year old Welsh woman, made Canvas House a very jolly place for high society by hosting endless parties and dances.

An elegant garden party at the New Fort, later called Stanley Barracks, built during the 1840's. The Old Fort or Fort York was situated to the northeast of this New Fort, c.1907.

During World War I, *Christie Pits* on the west side of Christie Street stretching from Bloor Street West to Barton Avenue, was re-named Willowvale Park.

The parks are for walking in, not for athletic sports and the streets for traffic, and woe to the boy who is caught desecrating them by playing there. A child of eleven years old appeared in police court charged with the offence of playing ball on Sumach Street. He was fined $2 or ten days in gaol. The child was doing nobody any harm and the city has something else to do with its money than pay policemen to run down children, who in their innocence, think it no sin to try and enjoy themselves.

from C.S. Clark, *Of Toronto The Good*, 1898.

Playing ball and going ankle dipping in Willowvale Park, c.1910.

EXHIBITION PARK.
RULES AND REGULATIONS.
THIS PARK IS OPEN TO THE PUBLIC
BETWEEN the following Hours
JUNE, JULY, AUGUST, 8 AM AND 8 P.M.
MAY, SEPT?, OCTOBER, 8 AM 7 P.M.
FROM 1ST NOV? to 1ST MAY, 8 AM 5 P.M.
EXCEPT during the holding of Exhibitions
and when the use of the Grounds are Granted
for SPECIAL PURPOSES.
Immoderate riding or driving, riding or driving
on the turf, injuring the trees or Buildings,
throwing Stones, or discharging firearms,
is STRICTLY PROHIBITED.
WAGGONS & CARTS not admitted.
PENALTY for INFRACTION
of these RULES & REGULATIONS, $50.
Toronto, BY ORDER JAS. CROMPTON.
MAY 17TH 1881. CHAIRMAN EXHIBITION COMMITTEE.

The Canadian National Exhibition (CNE), originally known as the Toronto Industrial Exhibition was founded in 1879 with agriculture as its basis. The CNE was situated on the actual location of old Fort Rouillé where the eighteenth century Frenchmen and the Indians first traded with each other. After the winter's hunt, the Indians would paddle down the network of lakes and portages toward Fort Rouillé where they would barter fox and beaver skins for bits of French clothing, combs, beads, mirrors and tin plates . . . the things that we pay for at today's CNE midway. The first CNE which was located beside the lake contained 23 wooden buildings and closed at dusk because there was no lighting. In 1912, the fair's name was changed to the Canadian National Exhibition.

The Canadian National Exhibition rules and regulations sign, 1881.

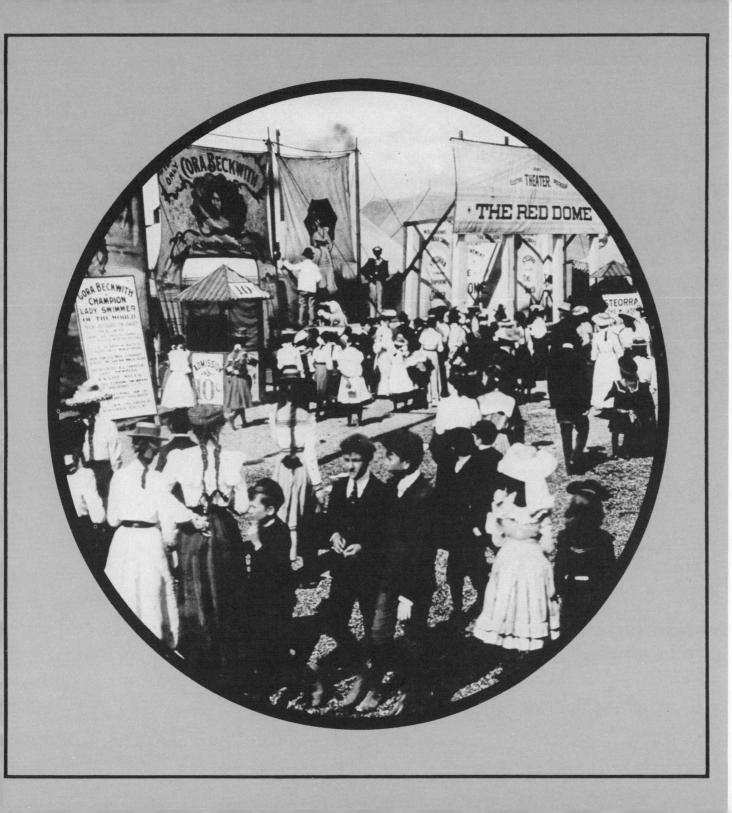

The Midway was designed by CNE directors in 1902 so that all the sideshows could be concentrated into one area. Some of the irresistible Midway attractions in 1906 included: Dr. F.R. Stewart and his Infant Incubators, L.T. Walters and the Laughing Gallery, Stuart Taggard and his Oil Painting entitled *Guilty*, and Mrs. W.H. Sibley with her Gorilla.

The Midway at the Canadian National Exhibition, c.1904.

Barnie Oldfield felt tense and ex-cited as he hunched over the wheel surrounded by throngs of well-wishers. And away he drove in the first racing car at the CNE.

Today the CNE,
Tomorrow the Grand Prix . . .

Car racing at the Canadian National Exhibition, c.1905.

Because all sorts of inventions were displayed at *the Ex* people thronged there anticipating the novelties of the times, such as the first electric streetcar in America, the first telephone, and the first moving pictures. In 1879 there were competitions for 20 different varieties of apples. In 1883, Consumers' Gas tried to show Torontonians that gas street lights could outshine electric bulbs. An early roller coaster called the Scenic Auto-Dip, the Daughters of Canada singing *The Maple Leaf Forever* and a lecture probing the question, "Does a tea-room pay? Yes!" were all big-time attractions.

The Women's Building at the Canadian National Exhibition with not a woman in sight, 1909.

What we today call the Toronto Islands was once a peninsula jutting out of Toronto Bay. Elizabeth Simcoe, wife of Governor John Graves Simcoe, was one of the first white people to discover the delights of the Islands' beaches, woods and picturesque lagoons. For centuries, the Indians had regarded the Islands as a place of healing and went there to restore their energies.

Governor Simcoe made the first official use of the Islands when he built a lighthouse on Gibraltar Point in 1808 which he regarded as a valuable part of the town's defences.

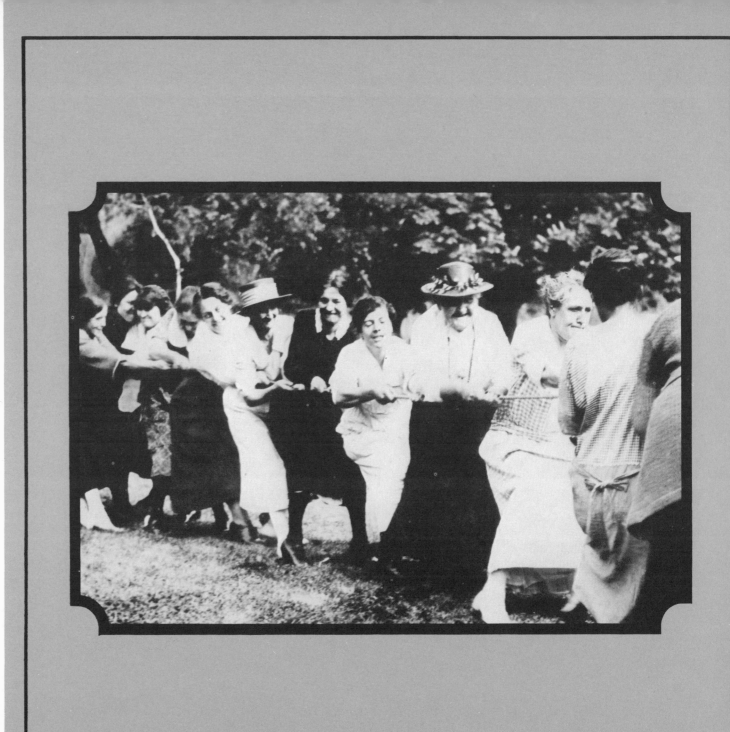

Centre Island picnic, the scene of the granny's tug of war, 1910.

The Island deserves to be reckoned in the very first rank of the suburbs of our city. The establishment of a magnificent public bath, the erection of a health home for sick children, the determination to enforce temperance, the multiplication of handsome private residences, the preparation for setting aside a people's park, all are indications that Toronto is at last beginning to appreciate her capabilities for beauty and healthfulness.

from C.P. Mulvany, *Toronto Past and Present*, 1884.

Centre Island, the scene of the highly competitive baby contest, 1909.

On the sands are bare-legged lads and lassies digging with wooden spades, building sand castles and wading in the shallow water. Under the trees and on the hotel porticos are bevies of young ladies, glorious in summer bonnets and holiday costumes. The Islands are evidently to Toronto what Coney Island is to New York.

from C.P. Mulvany, *Toronto Past and Present*, 1884.

Splashing about near Centre Island, c.1907. (above)

Centre Island, the scene of elegant ankle dipping and splashing about, 1909. (below)

A great step in advance for the Island has set in. A few years before, there had been a great deal of rowdyism, not only on weekends, but on Sundays. The bars and groceries were crowded with the lowest class of roughs. Near these haunts it was not safe for a lady to venture. Several of the worst outrages in the city's criminal records were committed by parties of men and women from Toronto in boats well-furnished with liquor. At length, a year ago, some improvement was affected in the personnel of the City Council of Toronto and a by-law was passed withdrawing all liquor licenses from the Island.

from C.P. Mulvany, *Toronto Past and Present*, 1884.

Posing for a family photograph on the Island, 1910.

Win? Place? Show? Lose?

The Dufferin Race Track was founded by the prominent Denison family who had received grants of land from the Crown because of their outstanding service to *King and Country*. It was Charles Leslie Denison who built the training course, but then took his horses somewhere else to run.

In 1908, with only 35 horses to operate a meet, Dufferin was officially opened. Whenever the race went late and darkness began to descend, the judges had to use lanterns to see the horses' numbers as they crossed the finish line. Dufferin was the first track in Canada to introduce the starting gate and the first to use a camera to assist the judges.

Open air betting at the Dufferin Race Track, c.1910.

Toronto is an out-of-doors city. All through the long spring and summer evenings, made longer by the stultifying of the clocks, the parks are crowded by muscular young men and maidens crying *Love Fifteen*, or *Vantage Out*. Baseball allures the boys and even transforms many girls into strange amazons with set expressions, long-peaked caps and expansive serge bloomers. Yachtsmen and dinghy sailors lie well out to windward. Pretty girls loll in canoes allowing their esquires the pleasure of paddling. Elders in white trousers trot down the lawn to watch the bias of the bowl and sporting golfers come breezing up the hill to the nineteenth hole with their tongues hanging out.

from J.E. Middleton, *Toronto's 100 Years*, 1934.

Lawn bowling in Alexandra Park, Dundas and Bathurst Streets area, 1909.

Seventeen magnificent golf courses are barely sufficient for the army of Toronto men and women who can spare time and money for the links, and the tennis players are numbered by the thousands.

from J.E. Middleton, *Toronto's 100 Years*, 1934.

Golfing, 1894. (above)

Golfing, 1907. (below)

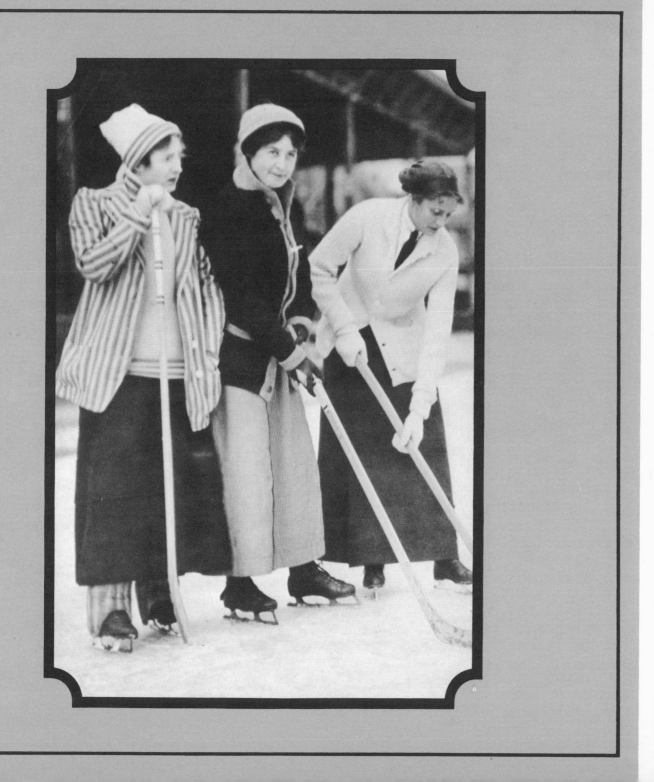

In 1877, women were allowed to take local examinations making them eligible for university entrance, and four years later, scholarships were established for them. In 1844, nine women entered the undergraduate program at the University of Toronto. Organized athletics for men began at the University of Toronto in 1885. Because the season for cricket and lacrosse ended in the fall, the chief game was football. The original football game played was known as the *old University game* and the *U. of T. Yearbook* of 1866 says that "charging from behind, hacking and tripping were prominent features. Players were not allowed to carry the ball, but they might bounce it along the ground with the hand." No other clubs, however, played football this way, and matches with teams outside the university were impossible.

Women students playing hockey at Varsity Stadium, University of Toronto, 1910.

Men are only apparently leaders. Close scrutiny will reveal a woman's power, a woman's encouragement, a woman's love and a woman's hand behind them.

from G. Nichols, *The Great Nineteenth Century Household Guide*, 1894.

Tennis, anyone? c.1907.

Toronto is a delightful place to live in. Its boating is unsurpassed. The bay on a summer night is one mass of skiffs and sail boats. There is scarcely a youth in the city who has not experienced the delights of rowing.

from C.S. Clark, *Of Toronto The Good*, 1898.

Paddlers at the Balmy Beach Canoe Club, c.1909.

In later years, as the city grew wealthier and more populous, the Island became not only a sanitarium, but a popular place of summer residence. Neat cottages, bungalow-like Bohemian dwellings of all shapes and dimensions as well as comfortable aristocratic villas lined the shore.

from C.P. Mulvany, *Toronto Past and Present*, 1884.

In Toronto, like all cities of pretentions, Sunday is a day of rest, but in practice it is the very reverse. The morning is usually devoted to church-going. There is a halo of respectability surrounding him who goes to church which nothing else can give. But those who are impervious to the refining influences of church attendance go down to their boat houses and prepare for the afternoon sail, or others go to the Island, there to remain during the day.

from C.S. Clark, *Of Toronto The Good*, 1898.

The don't drop it *egg and spoon race at Hanlan's Point on Toronto Island,* 1907.

There's more than one way to make a young girl behave in Miss Beaton's swimming class. It was either sink or swim!

Let any girl of eighteen or as young as twelve appear on Yonge Street after dark and her reputation is assumed to be light. In the course of her promenade, she will be spoken to and followed by scores of young men and boys who do not believe that young ladies of respectability appear on the streets after dark in the beautiful and saintly city of Toronto.

from C.S. Clark, *Of Toronto The Good*, 1898.

Miss Beaton's swimming class at the YWCA, 21 McGill Street, 1908.

Cuz it's one, two, three strikes you're out . . .

The Hanlan's Point Stadium was destroyed by fire in 1903. It was rebuilt and destroyed again by fire in 1909. A new stadium was constructed the following year and used by the International League Toronto Maple Leafs until they moved to Maple Leaf Stadium at Bathurst and Fleet Streets where they played from 1926-1967. In 1977, the Toronto Blue Jays began to *play ball* at Exhibition Stadium.

Baseball began in Toronto about 1875 with two semi-professional clubs known as the Dauntless and the Clippers. In 1885, a Canadian league was formed including teams from Toronto, Hamilton, London and Guelph. The Toronto players struck out at the salary of $4,231.42 per season.

Playing baseball at the Hanlan's Point Stadium on Toronto Island, c.1910. (above)

An unimpassioned baseball crowd at the Hanlan's Point Stadium on Toronto Island, c.1910. (below)

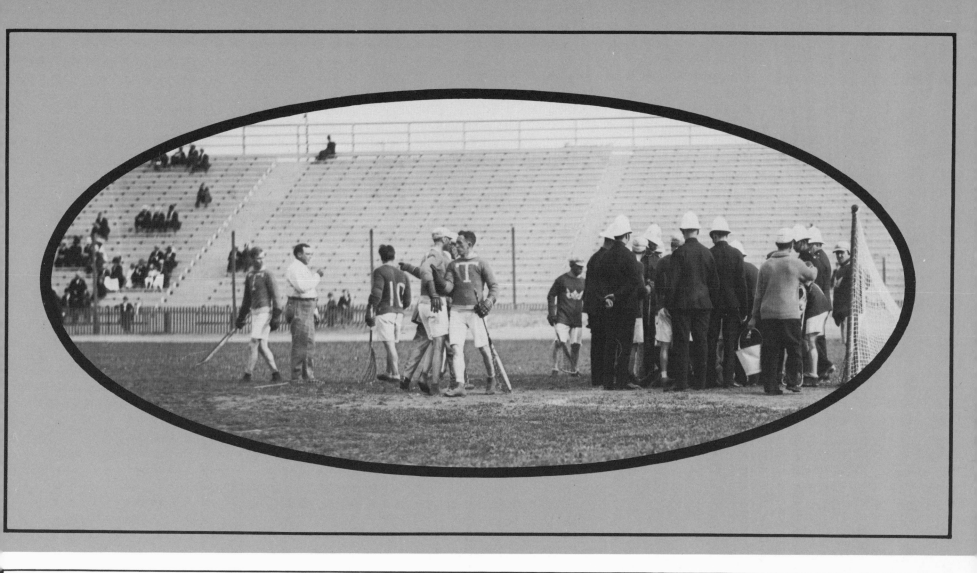

The progress of the game was rapid. In 1876 an association was formed including Toronto, Montreal, Ottawa and Cornwall. The players' enthusiasm expressed itself in undue roughness, and the managers' enthusiasm expressed itself in frequent protests, quarrels and withdrawals.

from J.E. Middleton, *Toronto's 100 Years*, 1934.

George Massey started the Toronto Lacrosse Club in 1867. Wearing knickerbocker uniforms, topped off with white caps, the team practiced in Queen's Park and played on cricket grounds before purchasing its own grounds in Rosedale. The team was very successful and often won the world championship. In 1867, it was argued that lacrosse should be recognized as Canada's national game. "Just as we declare the rivers, lakes and lands, once Indian-owned, to now be Canadian, so we now claim the Indian field-game to be the national field-game of this Dominion".

Playing lacrosse at the Hanlan's Point Stadium on Toronto Island, with a little help from our police, 1910.

J.W. GORMAN'S
DIVING HORSE
THE WHITE BEAUTIES
KING AND QUEEN

What a way to make a living!

Hanlan's Point, located at the tip of Toronto Island, was named after Edward *Ned* Hanlan, World Champion Oarsman, who was born in Toronto in 1855. When he was a small boy, his father moved the family to Toronto Island. In 1871, Edward was one of a crew which rowed in a race across Toronto Bay, and by 1876, he was the Champion Oarsman of Ontario. He then honoured his city and country by winning the World Championship in sculling.

Edward Hanlan's popularity, which naturally arose in the city where he added the distinction of being the champion oarsman of the world, drew attention to the comfortable luxurious hotel which he built at the western part of the Island fronting the city.

from C.P. Mulvany, *Toronto Past and Present*, 1884.

Mr. Gorman's diving horse at Hanlan's Point on Toronto Island, c.1907.

4

How we got there

Although this photograph may not show it, no other road in Toronto is so full of tradition and romance as the Lakeshore Road which runs along the city's waterfront. The Lakeshore Road which now transports thousands of cars, trucks, people and materials every day was once part of the old road from Quebec to Detroit. Before that, it was the route of postmen and dispatch carriers travelling between settlements, and even before that, it was part of the old Mississauga Trail which the Indians had blazed out of the wilderness.

The Lakeshore Road between Humber Road and Sunnyside Avenue, c.1910.

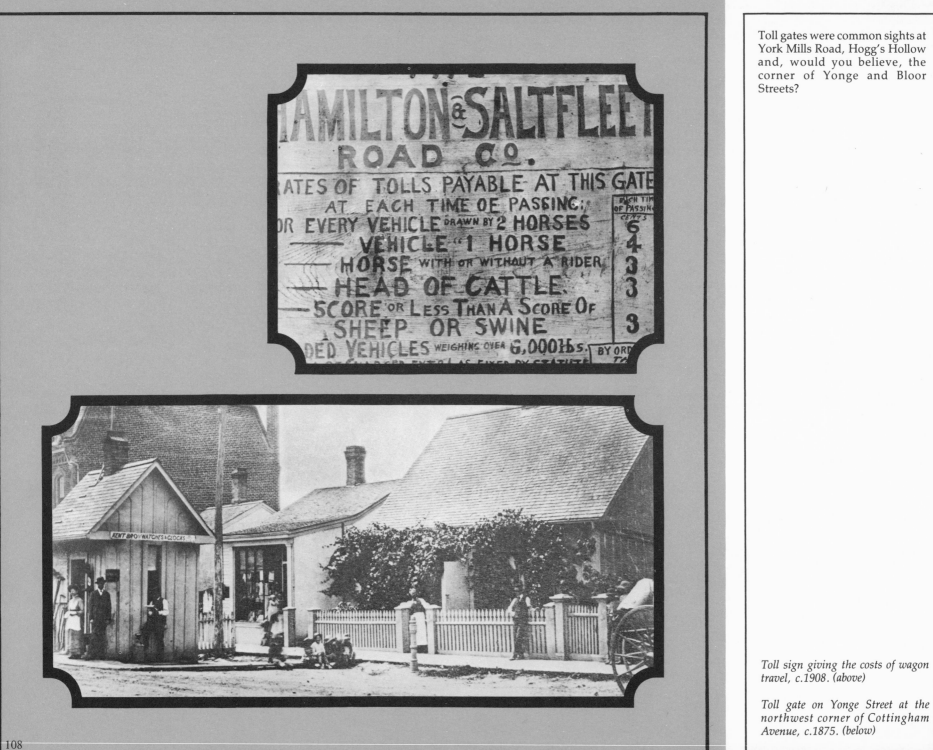

Toll gates were common sights at York Mills Road, Hogg's Hollow and, would you believe, the corner of Yonge and Bloor Streets?

Toll sign giving the costs of wagon travel, c.1908. (above)

Toll gate on Yonge Street at the northwest corner of Cottingham Avenue, c.1875. (below)

One could be happy here if one could tolerate the flies and frogs in summer and the relentless, iron winter.

from the diary of Anna Jameson, wife of Attorney-General Robert Sympson Jameson, 1836.

Trudging through the shoulder-high snow on Cherry Street, 1909.

A little, ill-built town, on low land, at the bottom of a frozen bay, with some government offices built of staring red brick in the most tasteless, vulgar style imaginable, three feet of snow all around and the grey, sullen wintry lake, and the dark gloom of the pine forest. I did not expect much but for this I was not prepared.

from the diary of Anna Jameson, wife of Attorney-General Robert Sympson Jameson, 1836.

The mud and the wind on the Weston Road hill, 1909.

Stuck in the mud?
Let them eat cake . . .

Making an ideal bread delivery in the Earlscourt area, 1909.

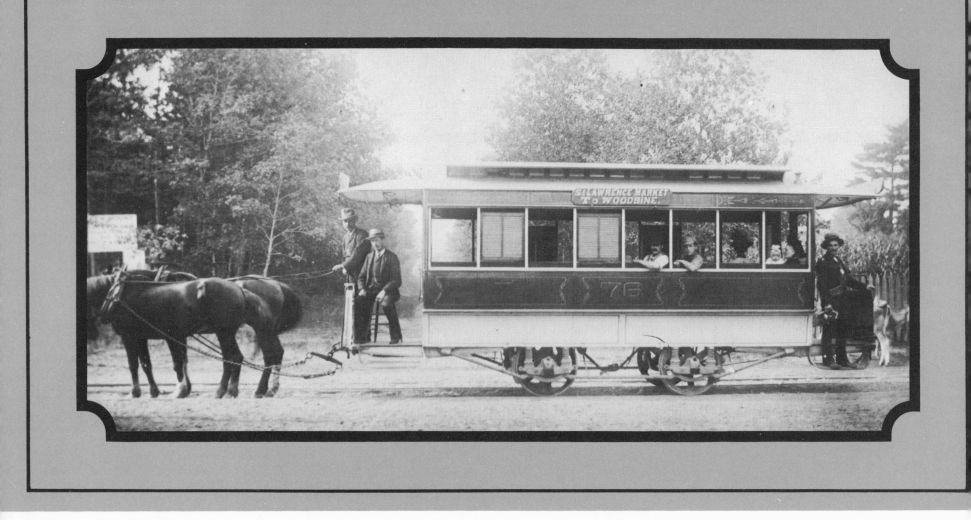

In 1861, a new method of transportation had arrived. The old lumbering omnibuses had been replaced by horsecars and Yonge Street was honoured with the first streetcar line in Canada. Some horsecars carried 16 passengers and were drawn by one strong and weary horse; others carried 24 passengers and were drawn by two strong and weary horses. These horsecars travelled on rails from the St. Lawrence Market to the Yorkville Town Hall. Anyone wanting to travel further north had to transfer to a stage coach or walk. The cars travelled at the unbelievable speed of six miles per hour. For 25¢, adults got six rides and children got ten. Because people could board at the front or the back of the car, honesty was the best and only policy.

A two-horse horsecar which ran from the St. Lawrence Market to the Woodbine Park area, c.1870.

In all kinds of weather, the conductors of these horsecars sat out in the open. Because the cars were unheated, conductors kept their feet in a box of straw to keep them from freezing. Straw was also placed on the floor inside the car to provide warmth for passengers' feet in the winter. During the summer, the horsecars operated 16 hours every day, but only 14 hours during the winter and, of course, never on Sunday. When roads became too treacherous, sleighs were used. In 1861, the horsecars transported 2,000 passengers a day and by 1891, they were transporting 5,000 passengers a day.

A one-horse horsecar which ran along King Street and up Spadina Avenue to Seaton Village in the Bloor and Bathurst Streets area, c.1898.

113

In 1890, the first electric streetcar appeared at the super speed of 12 m.p.h. Unfortunately, the old horsecar rails couldn't cope with the weight of these heavier cars and, combined with the cold weather and frost, the result was too many broken rail bonds. And so, the old reliable horsecars once again appeared on the streets. While this traumatic transition to and from electric cars was being made, the harried conductor often left his car to help his fellow-driver calm his frightened horses. In 1892, the controversy concerning electric streetcars prompted this outcry: "What will be the result of the trolley's application to King, Queen and Yonge Streets? The trolley will drive off carriages, decrease the value of property and increase danger to life. It is a mistake to accept it and will be a curse when it does come."

Typical Yonge and Albert Street traffic comprised of bicycles, horses and wagons, electric streetcars and pedestrians, 1908.

The Queen's Plate race which is run at Woodbine Park was inaugurated by the Prince of Wales in 1860. Although it is only a gift of fifty sovereigns, the honour is much coveted and generally brings out a good field besides giving an assurance of something like square dealing. The race was one of the finest ever witnessed in Toronto due in great measure to the admirable arrangements of the steward in securing order and suppressing the sale of liquor.

from *Canadian Illustrated News*, 1876.

Streetcars ready to take the hopefuls to Woodbine Race Track, c.1910.

In 1890, the officials of the Grand Trunk Railway were presented with a unique idea. Because communication across Canada was limited and very slow, Charles Carpmael, director of the Meteorological Department in Toronto devised an ingenious method of supplying farmers with weather forecasts to help them care for their crops and guide them in plowing and harvesting. Carpmael's idea was to have banners attached to the sides of the express cars of the Grand Trunk Railway trains. These banners would broadcast the weather as the trains travelled across the country. For example, a star on the banner would indicate that thunderstorms and rain were on the way, and the farmers should make proper preparations. The railway officials totally cooperated and so began Canada's, and the world's, first weather broadcast.

The Grand Trunk Railway Station at the foot of Yonge Street, c.1907.

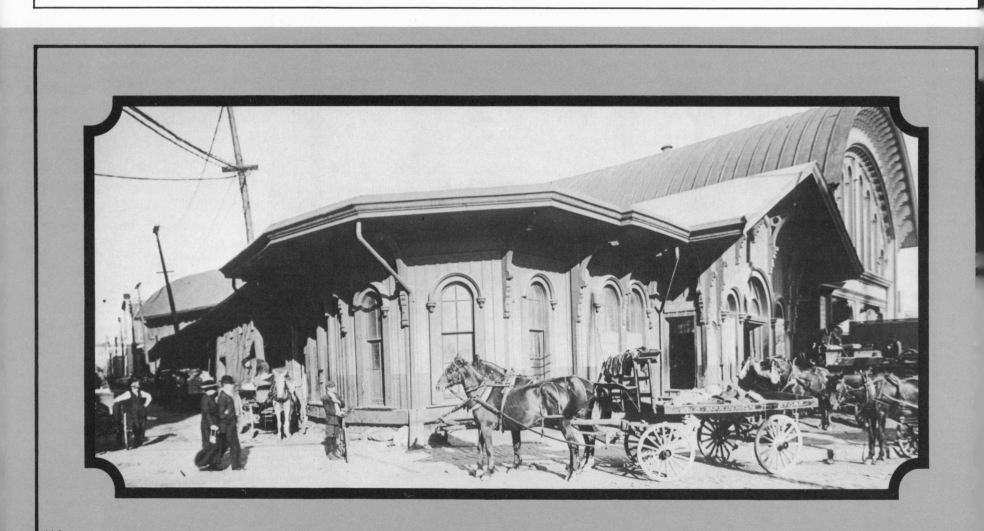

The legitimate business in Toronto is greater than that of any other place in Canada except Montreal. The city is the centre of Ontario commerce and offers the greatest advantages to persons engaged in trade. Merchants from a distance buy whatever they can here and thus combine business with pleasure. They like the liberal and enterprising spirit which characterises the dealings of Toronto wholesale men. They can buy here on better terms than elsewhere, and their relations with the merchants are satisfactory and pleasant. Everything gives way to business.

from C.S. Clark, *Of Toronto The Good,* 1898.

Doing business at the Yonge Street dock, 1907.

On December 8, 1869, Timothy Eaton opened his dry goods store at 178 Yonge Street at Queen Street. It was a three-storey building with a frontage of 24 feet and a purchase price of $6,500. On opening day, he employed two clerks and a small boy to wrap parcels. At the door were baskets of bargains including spools of thread which sold for 1¢ each. In 1877, he bought his first pony delivery wagon. So successful was business, that six years later he moved to 190 Yonge Street. The Eaton's philosophy of ''a square deal to everybody, the people to whom we sell and the people who work for us'' was obviously working. Because Mr. Eaton was a Methodist of stern conviction, his store never sold tobacco or playing cards.

One of the many delivery trucks belonging to the T. Eaton Co. Ltd. department store, c.1905.

The King Edward Hotel, opened in 1903, was one of the first public places in Toronto where women sipped alcoholic drinks, indifferent to whom might be watching. From its opening, the *King Eddie* catered to royalty, aristocracy, showbusiness people, financiers and just plain folk. Because many guests were known for their powerful thirsts, the hotel was liberal with its libations. At 15¢ a drink, a bottle of whiskey was placed on the table and left there until the guest had enough or too much. Architect E.J. Lennox, who designed Casa Loma and the old City Hall designed the hotel for W.G. Gooderham, the original owner. With its high-beamed ceilings and chandeliers, the elegant Victoria Room was a very popular dining spot. And no wonder . . . the 1908 menu served lobster for $1.50 and sirloin steak for 85¢.

Sitting in a brand new car in front of the King Edward Hotel on King Street East, c.1906.

119

Many of the photographs in this book were taken by William James, the first president of the Canadian Photographers' Association. In 1906, Mr. James emigrated to Canada from England with his wife and five children. They landed at Quebec City and then moved to Toronto where they lived at several residences in the downtown area on such streets as Huron, Major and Manning. William James was a superb photographer whose work often appeared in *The Toronto Star*. He died on November 18, 1948.

The children of photographer William James driving along the Toronto streets, 1910.

The first automobile, or motor carriage as it was often called, appeared on the roads as early as 1898. The Good Roads Association was formed in 1894 to encourage better road construction and maintenance. In 1904, motor vehicle licenses were first issued by the province of Onatrio and in that year, there were 535 passenger cars but no commercial vehicles or motorcycles. Driving a car always meant wearing goggles, bringing along the duster and being brave enough to mount the loose sand on Bloor Street near High Park and crossing the swamps on north Yonge Street. If you really wanted to get there . . . you still had to use your horse!

We are not amused! c.1900.

We are off, off into Toronto Bay and soon the wide expanse and cool breezes of Lake Ontario. As we steam out a mile or so, we get a pretty view of Toronto from the blue foreground of the waters — the whole rising spread of the city, groupings of roofs, trees, hills in the background. Goodbye Toronto with your memories of an agreeable visit.

from *Walt Whitman's Diary in Canada*, 1885.

Riding the swan boat across Toronto Bay, 1907. (above)

Taking the prop-driven sled across Toronto Bay, c.1910. (below)

Motorcar manufacturing in Toronto dates back to 1899 when the Canada Cycle and Motor Company (CCM) built a number of small motor tricycles and quadricycles for the post office. Although they were awkward in design, these single-cylinder, air-cooled machines performed well. In 1905, CCM (later the Russell Motor Car Company) produced a two-cylinder passenger car known as the Russell, named after the company president Tommy Russell. The very rich and daring immediately fell in love with the Russell which was fitted by hand, from crankshaft to shiny brass knobs to carbide headlamps. Soon more and more people began buying cars and living a life full of excitement, comfort, and, when all was running well, easier mobility.

Watching the airflights at Weston from the comfort of the automobile, 1910.

Although motorbikes and bicycles were very popular, nevertheless the proper way to call on a lady at a good address — Jarvis Street, St. George or Queen's Park — was behind a coachman and high-stepping pair of horses, carrying a black silk parasol in summer or bundling in buffalo robes in winter.

On a bicycle built for one, 1908.

The Globe was totally against any frivolity on Sunday, be it the running of streetcars or the pursuing of pleasure. In its holier-than-thou attitude which comforted generations of self-righteous Torontonians, the paper editorialized:

A number of youths were enjoying themselves playing *shinty* yesterday on Clare Street. His worship the mayor saw their proceedings and ordered the constable to arrest them. If the law is broken, the offender should be punished as a warning to others. Twenty-four hours in the cells would be a good means of stopping boys from practises of this kind on the Sabbath.

The royal procession on Major Street, c.1910.

Going my way? 1907.

It is pleasant to see that the last several reports of Mr. James Hughes, the vigilant gentleman who fills the important post of Inspector of Public Schools, show a marked improvement in the punctuality and attendance of the pupils at our city schools.

from C.P. Mulvany, *Toronto Past and Present*, 1884.

5

How we lived

Don't be afraid to go out-of-doors because it is a little colder than usual. The cold air will not hurt you if you are properly protected and take enough exercise to keep the circulation active. On the contrary, it will do you good. It will purify your blood, strengthen your lungs, improve your digestion, and energize your whole system.

from G. Nichols, *The Great Nineteenth Century Household Guide*, 1894.

Ontario Street south of Sydenham Street, after the snow storm, 1896.

Toronto's first water works was established by a private company in 1841. The city began providing the water supply to its citizens in 1873.

To supply our city with pure water was a hygenic grievance for many years. The water works were at an insufficient elevation and the supply, obtained from a part of Toronto Bay was too liable to contamination by sewage. The present water works are beautifully situated on a hill north of Toronto, where a miniature lake of nine acres, floored and walled with stone, serves as a reservoir. The grounds are beautifully kept and overlook the Mount Pleasant Cemetery. No visitor to Toronto should omit visiting the water works.

from C.P. Mulvany, *Toronto Past and Present*, 1884.

Resorting to waterworks carts when the water pipes were broken, York and Adelaide Streets, 1893.

In the early part of 1895, three disastrous fires occurred in Toronto's downtown area. On January 6, *The Globe* building at the corner of Yonge and Melinda Streets was practically destroyed and serious damage was done to the sites in the neighbourhood. Four days later, The Osgoode Building on Melinda Street was destroyed. On March 3, the new Robert Simpson Company store on the corner of Yonge and Queen Streets was practically burned to the ground. The total loss of these three fires was $1,645,153.

The fire at the Canadian Feather and Mattress Company at Melinda and Bay Streets, May 9, 1905.

131

On the evening of April 19, 1904, Toronto's most disastrous fire began in the E. and S. Currie neckwear factory on the north side of Wellington Street off Bay Street. The cause was attributed to a defect in the electrical wiring system and the strong winds blowing that night only aggravated the already grave situation. Firemen came by train from Hamilton, Niagara Falls, Buffalo, Peterborough, Brantford and London bringing their equipment on flat cars. But despite all their valiant human efforts, the pressure in the fire hyrants remained very low. By midnight, the area south of Bay and Melinda Streets, east to Front and Yonge Streets and west to the Queen's Hotel (later called the Royal York) was all in uncontrollable flames.

The aftermath of the Toronto Fire, Bay and Wellington Streets, 1904. (above)

The ruins of the Toronto fire, Bay Street looking north to the City Hall, 1904. (below)

On the morning of April 20, 1904, downtown Toronto resembled a bombed-out city in wartime.

The fire that had begun the evening before had consumed 14 acres of valuable, core land, as well as 86 buildings. The losses reached over $13,000,000 and the insurance amounted to $8,885,000. Five thousand people suddenly found themselves out of work. The offices and stock of companies dealing in paper products, such as Copp Clark and W. J. Gage, were completely destroyed. As *The Toronto Star* described it, "The fire ate millions in property, but no one was killed."

Examining the aftermath of the Toronto Fire, 1904.

Queen's Weather was what Torontonians called the warm sun that shone down upon them on the afternoon of June 22, 1897. They lined the streets, crowded the trolleys, decorated their shops and homes in honour of Queen Victoria, the glorious monarch who for fifty years, held one-quarter of all the people in the world under her command. The headline on *The Mail and Empire* read: ''Elaborate Decorations Testify to the Loyalty of the People.'' The Robert Simpson Company sold special Jubilee cushion covers made of genuine sateen with the Queen placed regally in the centre for the special price of 20¢.

On King Street East, Toronto celebrates Queen Victoria's Jubilee, 1897.

On the afternoon of Thursday October 10, 1901, Duke and Duchess of Cornwall and York arrived at a special station in North Toronto. Thousands of school children under the direction of Mr. A. Cringan, sang a patriotic welcome, despite the pouring rain. The Royal Party was then escorted in grand procession to the City Hall. The total amount of money spent by the city for this royal welcome was $10,623.76, without counting the thousands spent by private citizens in decorating and illuminating their shops and homes.

The Duke and Duchess of Cornwall and York arriving at City Hall, 1901.

On October 25, 1899, while bands played and Union Jacks waved, thousands of impassioned Torontonians lined the streets to say goodbye to the men who were now soldiers in Queen Victoria's regiments and off to fight in one of the most remote outposts in the world — South Africa. *The Toronto Star* printed, on the front page, the name of every man who passed his fitness test. The paper's social notices recorded each farewell party, and its regular feature column, *Topics for the Tea Table,* wrote: "Tonight sisters will cling to brothers bidding them stay, even as they push them away. Tonight lovers will stand with dulled eyes, teeth clenched and lips set hard."

Excited Torontonians welcoming the troops home from the Boer War, Bay and Temperance Streets, 1900.

To honour the Torontonians going off to fight the Boers on behalf of the British Empire, the Grand Trunk Railway offered return fare to Quebec to see the contingent sail for the price of the single fare. One enterprising merchant advertised his gas fixtures with patriotism: "The pick of our boys are off to lighten the dark of South Africa. Some of us are left behind to lighten the homes of Toronto. Call in and see us." Mayor John Shaw praised "the high imperial destiny of the British race and the righteousness of their cause." Many churches condemned the war, denouncing the Boers as selfish, cruel and unjust. One year later, on November 5, 1900, while bands played and Union Jacks waved, thousands of impassioned Torontonians welcomed *some* of the men back home.

Excited Torontonians welcoming the troops home from the Boer War, Yonge and Edward Streets, 1900.

A crowd of anxious, mostly male Conservatives (Tories) were waiting outside the offices of *The Evening Telegram* in anticipation of the election results of June 8, 1908. The spotlight shining from the window in this photograph reflected onto the blackboard which was placed in the newspaper's window. In these pretelevision days, this was the only way to give the crowds instant results. Similar groups of anxious, mostly male Liberals were waiting in anticipation outside the offices of *The Globe*. In 1918, Canadian and British women were granted the right to vote. American women were allowed this privilege in 1920.

Waiting for election results outside The Evening Telegram *building, Bay and Adelaide Streets, 1908.*

From July 8-August 8, 1912, the city of Toronto held a fly swatting contest. All competitors had to be Torontonians under 16 years of age. The first prize was $25 and the total prize winnings were $200.

This was certainly no fly-by-night contest! The rules were strict, the standards were high and the competition was keen. These flies were placed in pint bottles and measured by the city's Department of Public Health every Tuesday, Thursday and Friday before 5:00 p.m. Anyone found breeding his own flies or using any methods to make the bulk of his flies look bigger was instantly disqualified and irrevocably disgraced. A total of 66 girls and boys entered this contest and a grand total of 3,367,680 flies were killed.

Ladies and Gentlemen, meet Miss Beatrice White, the Champion Fly Swatter of the City of Toronto, 1912.

139

In 1881, it was found that horseracing had fallen to such a low ebb that some radical reforms became necessary. Leading horsemen of the day conceived the idea of forming the Ontario Jockey Club, with the view of placing horseracing on a proper footing. The institution is now flourishing, and the effects of its prosperity have been seen in the great increase of racehorses imported for racing and breeding, and the attendance of many people at races who, in times past, would not be seen on a race-course. The meets of the Club are held at Woodbine Park and so far, the races have been characterized with the utmost fairness.

from C.P. Mulvany, *Toronto Past and Present*, 1884.

Ladies, dressed to win, watching a horserace at the Ontario Jockey Club, Woodbine Park, c.1910.

In the 1900's, corsets were obviously a big and bulging business.

The Crompton Corset Company begun in 1876, was the first establishment in Canada to manufacture corsets on a large scale. The factory is a hive of industry, and employs 350 girls, some men and makes 8,400 corsets a week, as well as hoopskirts and bustles. Before that little thing that so aids in giving our women the beautiful figure that so many of them already have can be perfected, it undergoes fourteen processes. The embroidery designs emanate from the brain of one man who works with a delicate little French machine. The Crompton Company makes fifteen styles of corsets in sizes for young children of tender age to matrons with tendencies to *embonpoint*. In none of these corsets is whalebone used.

from C.P. Mulvany, *Toronto Past and Present*, 1884.

Dressed to win at the Ontario Jockey Club, Woodbine Park, c.1910.

In 1884, Dr. Canniff, Toronto's Medical Officer of Health, stated that large numbers of premises were without drainage, whereas many had defective drainage. This situation imperiled our citizens, causing and promoting disease. There were upwards of 500 cases in which neither city well or tank water was available. The massing of a vast number of human beings over a limited space, and the unhealthy vapours from stables and factories promoted typhoid and formidable diseases.

Squatters living on Toronto Island in their make-shift home, c.1908.

142

Until recently, pauperism has been little felt in this or any city of Ontario and we have been free from the squalor of the London slum. But during the last few years, the well-meaning authorities in the mother country, backed by our emigrant agents, have been committing the very serious error of sweeping into Canada emigration ships full of surplus paupers. The beggar and tramp are becoming only too familiar to Toronto streets. The girl and the boy outcast are in our midst. The question of organizing, or rather of controlling our public charities, is very pressing.

from C.P. Mulvany, *Toronto Past and Present,* 1884.

Hot night in the city slums, c.1910.

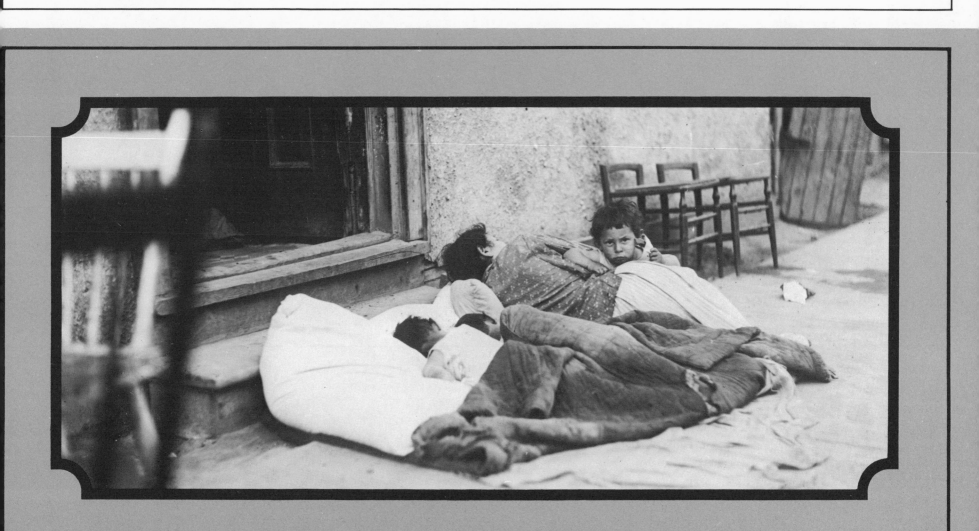

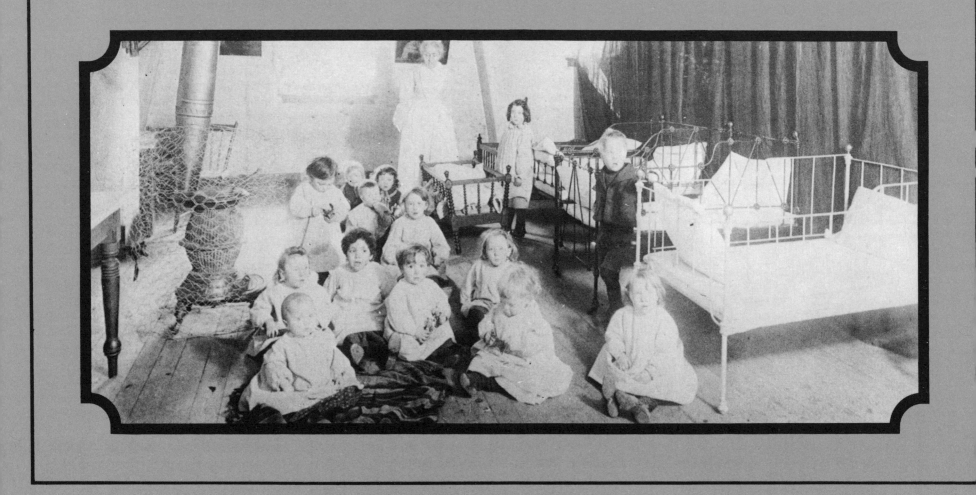

The physical conditions and development of the child depend upon the care and instruction of the parents. From the earliest infancy, children must have an ample supply of pure air. Keep the bedroom well-ventilated. Give children nourishing food, and until six years of age, they should live mostly upon a milk diet. Many young children suffer from overfeeding and care must be taken not to feed them too often.

from G. Nichols, *The Great Nineteenth Century Medicine Manual*, 1894.

The East End Day Nursery where the babies were kept, Dundas Street East between Sackville and Sumach Streets, c.1903.

In Toronto, poverty is not exactly a crime, but it is enough of an inconvenience to make everyone not desirous of possessing it. Here, money is the chief requisite.

from C.S. Clark, *Of Toronto The Good*, 1898.

You cannot always regulate the contents of your purse, but you can regulate the quality of your desires. Money is not within everyone's attainment, but contentment is. You are wealthy if you have learned two arts: first, how to be content with what you can get, and second, how to use what you have. If you want what 5¢ can buy and you have 10¢ then you are wealthy. A bright dime to a street child is greater wealth than a thousand dollars to a merchant prince.

from *The Complete Compendium of Universal Knowledge*, 1895.

The children of the streets, c.1910.

You can scarcely walk a block without your attention being drawn to the class called street boys. Every morning, rain or shine, summer or winter, a perfect swarm of them appear at the offices of different newspapers. Boarding the early streetcars, they deliver papers to all parts of the city. These lads are, as a rule, bright, intelligent fellows who would make good and useful men if they got a chance, but some are simply stupid. Some of them have no shoes, no coats and even their shirts are mere apologies. They can nearly all swim and enjoy themselves in summer, but the cold winter takes its toll upon them. Some of them live at home, but the majority are wanderers in the streets, selling papers or begging.

from C.S. Clark, *Of Toronto The Good*, 1898.

Slum children wandering the streets, c.1908.

Home! The name touches every fibre of the soul, and strikes every chord of the human heart. It recalls the fondest memories and opens the purest and deepest thoughts and feelings.

Home! The magic circle within which the weary spirit finds refuge. It is the sacred place to which the care-worn heart retreats to find rest from the toils of life.

Ask the lone wanderer as he plods his tedious way, ask him "What is home?" He will tell you, "It is an oasis in the memory, a centre about which the fondest recollections of the heart cling. It was once a glorious, happy reality, but now it rests only as an image of the mind."

from G. Nichols, *The Great Nineteenth Century Household Guide*, 1894.

A family dinner at the home of photographer William James, 1909.

Photographic Sources

THE CITY OF TORONTO ARCHIVES

The James Collection

page 8, 10, 15, 21a, 26, 36-40, 42, 45, 46, 49, 52, 55, 59b, 60-63, 65, 68-70, 73-81, 83-86, 89-104, 107, 108a, 109-117, 120-126, 139-147.

The City Engineer's Collection

page 23, 33, 50a, 53, 129, 132b, 133.

The Department of Public Works

page 50b.

METROPOLITAN TORONTO PUBLIC LIBRARY

page 3 (PC1867), 4 (E2-21B), 5 (B12-24C), 6a (E2-37E), 6b (E2-23B), 7 (B11-31B), 9 (E2-42B), 11 (B1373), 12a (E140B), 12b (E1-41A), 13 (*Art Work on Toronto.* Toronto: W.H. Carre & Co., 1898), 14 (X64-86), 16 (E1-42A), 17 (E3-2A), 18 (E4-71B), 19 (11-14B), 20 (X64-74), 21b (PC-1619), 22 (B10-8C), 24 (966-2-31A), 25 (Y-88), 27 (E1-27B), 28 (Y-30), 29 (X64-87), 30 (B12-20A), 31 (974-34-3), 32 (E4-87A), 34 and 36 (*Greater Toronto and the Men Who Made It.* Toronto: Inter-Provincial Publishing Co., 1911), 35a (968-12-565), 35b (E5-101C), 41 (977-32-5), 43a (976-30-2), 43b (974-4-7), 44 (977-19), 51a (B12-44B), 51b (B12-44A), 54 (971-20-4), 56 (B4-77C), 57 (B4-64A), 58 (971-20-1), 59a (973-1-15), 64 (X-64-83), 66a (964-4-2), 66b (964-4-5), 67 (964-4-4), 82 (967-2-14), 87 (968-8-7), 88 (966-1-7), 108b (E4-84C), 118 (X59-16), 119 (966-1-8), 130 (E5-103C), 131 (B4-92E), 132a (950-2-4), 134 (E2-15D), 135 (E5-5B), 136 (970-1-4), 137 (E2-48B), 138 (B10-36A).

Bibliography

Adam, G.M. *Toronto, Old and New.* Toronto: Coles Publishing Company Ltd., 1974.

Annual Report of the City Engineer's Department. Toronto: The Carswell Company, 1899.

Arthur, E. *Toronto, No Mean City.* Toronto: University of Toronto Press, 1974.

Balch, W.R. *The Complete Compendium of Universal Knowledge.* New York: Simalcrum Press, 1973.

Bédout, R. (ed.) *The Open Gate.* Toronto: Peter Martin Associates, 1972.

Clark, C.S. *Of Toronto The Good.* Toronto: Coles Publishing Company Ltd. 1970.

Davies, B. *Storied York Old and New.* Toronto: The Ryerson Press, 1931.

Dickens, C. *A Tale Of Two Cities.* U.S.A.: The Peebles Classic Library, 1976.

Duff, J.C. *Pen Sketches of Historic Toronto.* Toronto: J.C. Duff, 1967.

Filey, M. *Look At Us Now.* Toronto: M. Filey and *The Toronto Telegram,* 1971.

Filey, Howard & Weyerstrahs. *Passengers Must Not Ride On Fenders.* Toronto: A Green Tree Publication, 1974.

Filey, M. *A Toronto Album.* Toronto: University of Toronto Press, 1970.

Filey, M. *Toronto Reflections Of the Past.* Toronto: Nelson, Foster & Scott Limited, 1972.

Filey, M. *Trillium and Toronto Island.* Toronto: Peter Martin Associates, 1976.

Filey, M. *The Way We Were.* Toronto: Nelson, Foster & Scott Limited, 1976.

Guillet, E.C. (ed.) *Pioneer Inns and Taverns.* Toronto: Edwin C. Guillet, Publisher, 1954.

Harney, R. and Troper, H. *Immigrants.* Toronto: Van Nostrand Reinhold Ltd., 1975.

Hart, P.W. *Pioneering in North York.* Toronto: General Publishing Company Limited, 1968.

Kilbourn, W. *The Toronto Book.* Toronto: The MacMillan Company of Canada, 1976.

Lorimer, J. *The Ex.* Toronto: James Lewis & Samuel Publishers, 1973.

Middleton, J.E. *The Municipality of Toronto, Vols. I-II.* Toronto: The Dominion Publishing Company, 1923.

Middleton, J.E. *Toronto's 100 Years.* Toronto: The Centennial Committee, 1954.

Mulvany, C.P. *Toronto Past and Present.* Toronto: Coles Publishing Company Ltd., 1970.

Myers, J. *The Great Canadian Road.* Toronto: Red Rock Publishing Company , 1977.

Nichols, G. *The Great Nineteenth Century Household Guide.* Toronto: Coles Publishing Company Ltd., 1978.

Nichols, G. *The Great Nineteenth Century Medicine Manual.* Toronto: Coles Publishing Company Ltd., 1978.

Richmond, J. *Discover Toronto.* Toronto: Doubleday Canada Ltd., 1976.

Roberts, C.G.D. *Appleton's Canadian Guide-Book.* Toronto: George N. Morang and Company Ltd., 1899.

Robertson, J.R. *Robertson's Landmarks of Toronto, Vols. 1-5.* Toronto: John Ross Robertson, Publisher, 1894.

Scadding H. *Toronto Of Old.* Toronto: Adam, Stevenson & Co., 1873.

Schull, J. *100 Years Of Banking In Canada.* Toronto: The Copp Clark Publishing Company Limited, 1958.

Students of Toronto Island Public School. *A History of the Toronto Islands.* Toronto: The Coach House Press, 1972.

Wallace, W.S. *A History of the University of Toronto.* Toronto: University of Toronto Press, 1927.

Wayne, R. *Honest Womanhood.* Toronto: New Hogtown Press, 1976.